YOU CAN OVERCOME ANYTHING!

VOL.4

WHEN YOU WALK WITH CERTAINTY

CESAR R. ESPINO WITH CONTRIBUTING AUTHORS

WITH A SPECIAL CHAPTER BY

NICOLAS R. SRUT

CRE
COMPANIES

Published by Cesar R. Espino / CRE Companies

You Can Overcome Anything! Vol.4 / Cesar R. Espino With Contributing Authors

ISBN 978-1-7346995-4-8 (dBook)
ISBN 978-1-7346995-5-5 (pbk)

www.CesarRespino.com

DEDICATION

This book is dedicated to those who are looking to get inspired, motivated, and empowered. To those who walk with certainty regardless of the obstacles and keep marching forward to overcome those challenges no matter what. My faith is that you will find stories within these authors to help you on your own journey. In these stories you will find ideas and real-life lessons to show you how you too can truly Overcome Anything!

CONTENTS

ACKNOWLEDGEMENTS

I am thankful and grateful for each of the authors that have taken the time to share their story and are using their live lessons to inspire, empower, and motivate the readers.

I am honored to have each of the authors in this project and I want to acknowledge you:

Nicolas R. Srut
Lisa Manzo
Hershey Ann Duenas, MBA
Sarah Ferguson
Ann Wood
Sean Steiner
Carmen Ventrucci
Julie Williams
Guinevere Smith
Cally Stamp
Maggie Olson
Susy Elizabeth Ramirez
Christina Krag
Lisa Shawver
Pamela Grant
Cesar R. Espino, MBA

Thank you so much for your wealth of knowledge and for sharing the obstacles you had to overcome and how by walking with certainty you were able to overcome some challenges in your life journey. You are truly an encouragement and inspiration to the readers, **thank you!**

Nicolas R. Srut

CHAPTER ONE

LEGACY

Finally, it was time for her to be mine. *Finally,* I had mustered up the confidence to ask out the first girl I ever had a crush on.

Here we are. Sixth grade. Middle school. Picture little bald me, dressed in my snazziest blue button-down t-shirt, my cleanest jeans, and the coolest pair of Converse that my allowance could buy me, ready to ask out the girl who, in my young mind at the time, was the girl of my dreams. *My* Juliet, *my* Cinderella, *my* special lady to call my own. This was the *first time* in my life I cared about girls. My *first time* playing the game of "love."

Happy, confident, bald Nico straightened his collar and approached his soon-to-be girlfriend. Now, to clarify, I am bald because of my autoimmune condition known as Alopecia. Essentially, all Alopecia does is make you lose your hair. Other than that, you're perfectly healthy. Sometimes it's partial baldness, other times it's total baldness to where you look like you could be related to Mr. Clean. In my case, I'm rocking the confident eggshell every day.

With all that being said, let's go win our first girlfriend. I walked up to her, pep-in-my-step, no doubt in my mind, chin up high, and asked her the life-changing question, in a sophisticated fashion that only a middle-schooler could pull off:

"Do you wanna be my girlfriend?"

She looked at me for a few moments. A few moments of the loudest silence I had ever experienced. She chuckled a little bit.

Uh-oh.

She smiled - *that* smile. You know, the one where you know you aren't going to like the next words out of that person's mouth.

I stood there apprehensively, and then she said these exact words,

"I like you a lot, Nico. I just think I would like you more if you had **hair**."

Gunshot. My heart. My soul. Is that a—white light?

The first girl I ever wanted to ask out. The first girl that actually made my heart dance when I saw her—rejected me because I didn't have hair.

And when I tell you that from then on, for the longest time afterward, I assumed I *had* to have hair to be desirable—I tell you, I believed it with my entire heart. This incident, combined with hundreds of days in school of being called "cancer head" or "alien kid," being physically abused, to the point where one kid nearly broke my hand (and he would have, too, if one of my friends hadn't come to my rescue) were the overwhelming, suffocating, confidence-shattering reasons why I wore a wig for several years of my life.

For years, I allowed *other people* to control my life. For years, the shoes I was walking in were nail-filled shoes that made my toes bleed. Shoes that my greatest enemies *handed* me to wear. For years, I was an impostor. I was never farther from myself than when I wore that wig on my head.

But in those days, I thought it was my ticket into normalcy. I thought it was my one way to be loved and accepted. I thought those who physically and emotionally abused me would release their grip around my throat.

And when I gave them what I thought they wanted, it didn't even help. Not only that, but suddenly *I* was the one with my hands around my *own* throat.

I was anxious every day that the wig was going to come off while I was playing sports, anxious the boys in my class would try to rip it off (and believe me, they tried), distressed by the fact that suddenly my world revolved around something I had no control over.

When I gave into pleasing people, it actually made things WORSE.

Pause.

In those lessons of pain that I had, there are two realizations that have shaped the confident person I am today. The guy who lives for himself changes the world and is the reason millions of people around the world smile and laugh every single day.

Point one: I was trying to please everyone else but myself.

Being a people pleaser means neglecting your own happiness. And when I lost my happiness, suddenly I had no more happiness to give. Ironically, we believe that being a people-pleaser will help us make the people we care about happier, but the opposite comes true. When I allowed myself to make other people happy before myself, I grew bitter and depressed. And believe me, a depressed person has a *tough* time spreading happiness.

In a very fitting analogy, the best way I can put this is this: Imagine you're at a store that sells the world's best cookies. I mean, these cookies are fantastic. They *really* are the world's absolute best cookies. You wait in line for several hours, putting in the time and effort to get this cookie you can't wait to enjoy. Finally, you get the cookie, and right as you're about to enjoy it, your friends and family approach you. Everybody asks if they can have a piece of this amazing cookie that you waited in line and paid for. You're reluctant to give it up, but because you love them, you give them each a piece. Person after person, you keep breaking off small pieces of the cookie--until you're left with no cookie at all. Now, you're out $5, wasted hours in line, and you're upset because everyone else is enjoying the cookie *you* worked for. Think of the cookie as a metaphor for your mental well-being and energy. It stings even more that you're losing out because you have nobody to blame but *yourself*. You could have just told them, "I love you, but I waited and paid for this cookie, and I want to enjoy it." And that's perfectly fair. And then you get to enjoy what you worked for, your own mental well-being and energy, and you're made happier because of it.

Point two: I was trying to control those things I had no control over.

Here's a very simple analogy: You're walking over the middle of a train track out in the middle of a beautiful, mesmerizing, flower-studded wide-open field. Suddenly, you hear the train approaching you, *way too close* for comfort. This train represents the opinions of others, the crazy, insane, spontaneous hardships, tragedies, and mishaps in life that occur unexpectedly. It's everything that happens whether we want it to or not. You have two options as this train is approaching. Option one: get out of the way, let it roll by, and while you might spend some time hyperventilating, hands on your knees, looking down at the ground, in disbelief that you just had what felt to you like a near-death experience almost getting hit by the train--when you catch your breath, when you look up, you'll see that beautiful, mesmerizing, flower-studded wide-open field right in front of you. And suddenly you'll realize how little that train ultimately mattered. You get to enjoy your day, be free in the open field, and you'll soon entirely forget all about the train. And you've learned a valuable lesson: don't stand in the middle of train tracks. Option two: keep standing in the track and try to stop the multiton behemoth on wheels. We know how this story ends. So many things happen that are out of our control. The sooner we get out of the way and go stand in the open field rather than right in front of big, scary trains that can hurt us, the sooner we find our peace, happiness, and confidence.

When I tried to fight losing my hair, I was going to lose that battle no matter what. There is no cure for Alopecia. Wigs are only a way of covering up your baldness, but they made me feel inauthentic. I hated them for that. The day when I decided I was going to stop pleasing other people, enjoy the cookie I worked for, control those things I could, and let go of those that I couldn't--and just let that big heavy train pass me by--I truly took charge of my life.

I remember the day I made the absolutely mortifying decision to take off my wig, too. That was the day I felt the *most insecure* I ever had. But it was also the day I felt the *freest*. Only about a month later, after getting comfortable with my authentic person, putting myself first, and only concerning myself with those things I could control, I not only felt my most free, I felt my most confident.

And I still do today.

These two simple lessons are the foundation for everything that I do, and they can be applied to practically every situation. Work, school, intimate relationships, personal relationships with friends and family. You name it, and these principles will help you in it. They are centered around one simple idea: *giving your power away*. When you let things out of your control dictate your life, and you live to please everyone else, you have no power left. No energy. Taking your power back means living for yourself, focusing on what you can control, and taking full command of *your own life*. And when you're happy with yourself, happy with your direction, suddenly you have *so much* power and *so much* energy to pour into yourself and your life. With these two lessons, you become the person that *you want* to be, not the person everyone else wants you to be, and that, in turn, will lend you **unconquerable confidence.**

I wanted to share this story with you for two reasons. One, I hope that it will help you in your own life in some fashion. And two, it provides context for who I am today and how my mindset has catapulted me into achieving what I have today. I want you to see how mindset, and most importantly, *certainty*, led me to become an influencer who inspires and motivates millions of people every single day and how you can shape your mindset to guide you on your own path.

On June 4, 2020, I had my first viral TikTok video. It was a silly video where somebody called me out for not having any eyebrows, and I pretended to get "angry" about it. In the video, as I'm getting "angry," I draw on angry eyebrows with an Expo marker. It was super silly, and it showcased my confidence with my Alopecia. It demonstrated I was willing to do something most people would probably find humiliating, but instead, I made it funny.

It accumulated millions of views, and I ended up climbing from 3,000 followers to over 25,000 in just a few days.

But the sudden growth in following isn't what mattered to me.

However, what did matter to me was that someone else with Alopecia, whose name I'll leave anonymous out of respect for them and their personal journey, sent me a message on TikTok. He expressed how he had been wearing hats and fake eyebrows in public. He told me that my confidence was inspiring and that he wanted to get rid of his fake eyebrows and his hat and truly be himself in public, but he didn't know how.

I spent the next hour talking with him, pouring my heart and soul into every word, helping him build up the confidence to fully embrace his Alopecia. After that night, I didn't hear from him for a little while. I didn't know what to think.

And then a week later, he messaged me again. He told me that he stopped wearing his wig in public. He told me he got rid of his fake eyebrows. He thanked me for all of the advice I gave to him and said that if it wasn't for our talk, for the wisdom I gave to him, he wouldn't have been able to do it.

After he sent me that last message, I spent the next several minutes profusely crying tears of joy.

At that moment, I knew that was why I was going to pursue a career as an influencer.

When this revelation happened, I was with a very dear friend of mine. You know, the kind who really knows who you are. The one you can tell absolutely anything, and they truly understand you.

After reading that my new Alopecian brother had gotten rid of his fake eyebrows and hats, I turned to my friend and, with the utmost passion and confidence, almost like I was in a trance, I proudly stated, "This one video is leverage." This one viral video is *traction* that can lead me to where I've always wanted to be. I have the chance to keep this going and make more videos to keep helping more people to be confident in who they are. Not just people with Alopecia, but *people*! I've always wanted to do this, and now I have the chance. If anyone else was in the room with me right now, they wouldn't believe these next words out of my mouth. They wouldn't believe them because they go against everything they've been taught: that a one-in-a-million shot is basically impossible, but because it's you, I know you'll believe me: I am going to use this traction to keep my TikTok account growing. I am going to use this leverage to help more people to be confident. I'm going to change the world.

"And it's going to happen because I said it's going to happen."

I had never felt surer about anything in my life. I had never felt more certain about my direction.

At present, I was in my last semester of college before getting an associate's degree. I had to make one of the most difficult choices of my life that went against everything that I was taught. I knew that if I continued along my collegiate path and pursued a bachelor's degree, I would lose the traction I was building, and I wouldn't be able to give my media platform the time it deserved. As I was growing up, I was told that you need a bachelor's degree to be "successful." That in today's "competitive market," sometimes a masters or even *two* bachelors are even better. One: that might be true for some people, but I wasn't going to let that be *my* truth. And two: success is subjective. Society's common definition of success in America means to be wealthy. That's not mine. My definition of success is to wake up every day and love what I do. To never dread getting out of bed in the morning and rather spring out of bed every single day, excited to get to work. And, coincidentally enough, when you truly love what you do, you work harder at it, and thus you tend to make good money doing it.

I knew that I didn't need a degree. I was willing to risk it all, to take a leap of faith, and give being an Influencer all that I had in me. And, in throwing myself to the wolves, I knew that I would fight a million times harder to make it happen than if I had the safety net of college. Getting rid of my safety net meant I had to give this *everything I had* as if my life depended on it.

My decision not to continue pursuing my degree and focus on what *I already knew I could do* was the single greatest decision I ever made for my career.

When I started to build my platform, I really did give it *everything*. For 237 days in a row, never taking a weekend off, I would post an average of 8 videos a day on TikTok. I gave all of this effort with great joy. I was pursuing something that *meant* something to me. And on the days that it was difficult, when I would have a serious creative block, when I would get discouraged pouring in so much effort with little return, I would remind myself who I was doing it for. I wanted to be able to grow my TikTok to help show people how to be confident in their own skin, and *especially* to become a leader of the Alopecia awareness movement.

When I created my first viral trend, I was featured on the TikTok Trends Instagram page. It served as affirmation that I could do this, that I had what it takes to keep on growing.

About a month after my first viral trend is when I became a *viral meme*. If you don't know what a meme is, basically, it's kind of like an inside joke across all of the internet. People know of a certain joke or character or video from the internet, and they quote it in real life. Other people who know the meme will mimic the meme when someone else says it. Weirdly enough, in my generation, one of the ways we bond and make friends is actually *through memes*, so to become a meme is a big deal.

I became a viral meme and was referred to as "The PUEBES Guy." The backstory to the whole "PUEBES" thing is that on a video where I explained that I couldn't grow hair anywhere, some guy had this brilliant idea: What do you do on a public platform where a guy explains he can't grow hair anywhere? Ask him if he can grow pubes, of course! Except this gentleman didn't spell the word properly. He spelled it "puebes." Being that I'm bilingual, this word looked *very* Spanish to me. So, in a video replying to his comment, in my very best Duolingo-guy accent, I explained a whole story about my nonexistent PUEBES. That video went viral, and before I knew it, I began making a whole PUEBES series. The #puebes now has hundreds of videos, with hundreds of millions of views on TikTok. I had people in every country around the world saying PUEBES just like me. And funnily enough, this became the greatest way for me to connect with the Alopecia community I wanted to lead. I mean, to everyone else, it was funny, but you can imagine how much funnier it was to the people who knew *exactly* what I was talking about.

I used this viral leverage to create an Alopecia support group, where I mentor hundreds of people with Alopecia to this day, and *that's* what I'm the proudest of. I get to help *hundreds* of my people grow in their confidence and self-love and make a *real* difference in the world.

When the PUEBES meme brought a whole bunch of people to my TikTok and Instagram, I showed them I was more than just a meme and kept pushing out both comedic and inspirational videos.

Almost an entire year later when I'm writing this from my initial start on June 4, 2020, I sit at 5,000,000 followers on TikTok and a third of a million on Instagram. I am a speaker for national organizations for people with Alopecia, I am at the forefront of the Alopecia awareness movement where I always wanted to be, I have had the chance to work with numerous big-time brands, you can find me on famousbirthdays.com, and I get to be the reason that millions of people around the world laugh and smile every day.

What's more than that to me is the hundreds of messages I've received from people worldwide, from different backgrounds, from people who were struggling with insecurities of all kinds. They tell me how my videos have helped them to accept and love themselves more. My videos inspired them to stop giving in to pleasing other people, and that they are finally able to feel comfortable and confident in their own skin.

That's why I do it. The dream that I had not even a full year ago is my reality today. And I made it come true because I wanted it badly enough. I firmly believe that if you *really* want something badly enough, it's as good as yours. If you are willing to fight incessantly, no matter the setback, no matter how long it takes, you are going to have everything you've ever wanted. I honestly believe the reason people call things a "one-in-a-million chance" is because the only person who *makes it* is that "one-in-a-million" who decided to never give in, no matter how much their family, friends, or society, or any other naysayer told them they couldn't make it.

It's not that it's impossible to make it. It's that it's tough to persevere when you feel like you're against all odds. But you can only *be* against all odds if you *think* you are. So choose not to. Keep up with the pursuit of your own ambitions. **If you want it badly enough, you're going to get it.** *That* is all you need to think.

About the Author

Nicolas Roman Srut is a 21-year-old internet personality with over 5,000,000 followers across his TikTok and Instagram platforms. He has an autoimmune condition known as Alopecia which made him lose all of his hair. After years of being insecure about his baldness in his early life, he has transformed the confidence he now has into the comedic and inspirational content that motivates millions of people all across the world today. He has an organization known as The Naked Confidence Campaign, where he personally coaches hundreds of people with Alopecia to grow in their confidence and self-love. So far, he has helped numerous people get rid of their wigs, shave their patchy heads, ditch their fake eyebrows, and truly walk with Naked Confidence. He will soon transform The Naked Confidence Campaign into a live event that will be available to anyone, not just people with Alopecia, to learn to grow in their self-confidence, take charge of their lives, and change the beauty standards of society forever. You can follow him on TikTok and Instagram under the handle @xtheromanempire, and you can check out his website at www.thenakedconfidencecampaign.com

Lisa Manzo

CHAPTER TWO

SURRENDER AND ACCEPTANCE

"Never underestimate the power you have to take your life in a new direction." - Germany Kent

Perhaps, you are reading this chapter because of the title! The title came to me about three months into this journey. I was explaining what was going on in my head and my body to a friend. I was trying to figure out a way to describe it so she could understand! Then I remembered the movie, Mean Girls. In the movie, Lindsay Lohan's character says," Oh, no. It was coming up again, word vomit...." That is exactly what it felt like. So, instead of word vomit, I was experiencing emotional vomit. All these emotions were surfacing (depression, powerlessness, hopelessness, helplessness, worthless, rage, anger, doubt, overwhelm, frustration, irritation, and impatience). They were demanding to be acknowledged. The feelings came up and just kept coming. Sometimes one or two and sometimes five or six at the same time. I knew I had to experience the emotion in order to release it from my subconscious! Yet, I resisted.

It has taken me a long time to accept that I had to deal with these emotions before moving on. Specifically, the feeling of worthlessness! I felt the other feelings I have listed as well! Worthlessness was the dominating emotion for me! I'm working with someone to discover where this has come from. I must thank Tiffany Toombs for writing the book "Stop Being a Selfish Bitch." Tiffany, in her book, explains how these feelings have developed. It was very enlightening. It helped get me through my journey quicker. These emotions relate back to childhood and my child's mind not having the ability to cope with the events that occurred in my life. During my journey, I have come to understand that unresolved negative emotions get stored in the body. To release these emotions, you must feel them and allow them to be released from your body. I had to surrender to the journey of feeling my emotions. Wow! Haven't done that in years. I actually don't know how to feel my emotions anymore. I feel like this came from my generation when people didn't talk about their feelings because it made people uncomfortable.

When you think of surrender, what does it mean to you? When I first heard about surrendering, I thought people were crazy. What do you mean by surrender? I'm not giving up. I'm going to keep going on. I'm going to persevere. Then it was explained to me that surrendering did not mean giving up. It means surrendering to the journey that I have been brought here to accomplish. Let go of control and allow life to unfold with all the wonderful things life offers when you fully embrace life. To becoming the best version of me and fulfilling my life's purpose, whatever that may be. I say whatever that may be because I am working on becoming clear on exactly what that is. I have understood that I must let go and allow the journey to happen and release control. My friend, Edie O'Reilly, writes in her book, When the Body Speaks, that life is happening for you and not to you. My interpretation of that is that the things that are happening in my life, good or bad, are there for me to learn, grow, and evolve into the best version. It took me a while to accept this as true. When I was feeling my emotional vomit, I felt like the victim. Why me? Have you ever felt like that?

The change came when I started asking God or the Universe, (you decide what word works for you) for help. Then people started appearing in my life, and I watched as they transformed themselves, and I wanted the same for myself. As previously stated, Tiffany was the one who opened the door for my healing to begin. I began to let go of my past and the misery, whether the misery was perceived or real. This was when I learned that you must feel your emotional trauma to release it and move on in your life. This is no easy task. Yet on the other side of the journey, there is peace, joy, and contentment.

This made me curious about other people's thoughts on this topic. Below are a few answers to the question, "What does surrender and acceptance mean to you?"

Aras replies:

For me, surrender always has to come before acceptance. Surrendering to the fact that I simply don't know what is best for my life. I don't know how to manage and control my day whatsoever. I don't know how to manage and control my relationships, and I don't know how to manage and control my emotions. So, what am I surrendering to? I am surrendering my own will, because my life becomes disastrous when I have not surrendered. That's where God comes in for me in my life because surrendering, even though I don't think morning meditation and readings are going to fix me, I do it anyway because self-will has shown me that my shelf life without morning meditation, prayer, and readings is about 3 three days before I start making big messes. If I surrender and take action in prayer and take a look at my own behavior. I have an easier time with acceptance and accepting things that feel very inconvenient for me, like someone else's bad behavior. I don't want to accept that, but I certainly have to. Do I want to be right, or do I want to be free today? I really have to accept things that I may find objectionable in other people. If I surrendered, the beauty in that is that I can look at things from an entirely new perspective. I've to be in a position of neutrality, even though I may not like someone else's behavior, even though I may not like the results I am getting in my life, work, school, friendships. Acceptance allows me to sit in the position of neutrality. I can be uncomfortable and continue moving on through my day and still be in a place of serenity overall. Serenity is a position of neutrality, and I can do what I need to do. I am able to be useful to others.

Stacey replies:

Surrender is often thought of as giving up, quitting, or being weak to someone or something that's more powerful than you because you are defeated. Someone who surrenders is considered "weak." In a wartime situation, that may be the case. In fact, being able to "surrender" is being strong! It's the ability to let go of things you can't control, and this allows the person who surrenders to be open to receiving more. If you're holding onto something and then surrender it, it frees up your hands to accept something new. It's the same concept with emotional availability. When you surrender what's weighing your down, holding you back, or what you don't have control over, it leaves room for freedom to enter, and there will then be more possibilities! Acceptance is the ability to receive. You must surrender or "give up" what is holding you back or what you're holding tight onto in order to "accept" or receive what is meant to be yours! This is freedom!

L.A. replies:

I just know, acceptance is the answer to all my problems, and I have to surrender to win. Give up controlling and managing, and realize life is life, people are people, and the only life I can choose to dictate is my own!

Tuesday replies:

Surrender is an intentional act of letting go of a held belief, idea, or feeling and allowing the natural course of things, be the ultimate decision decision-maker as to all outcomes. Let go and let God. Acceptance is a repeated effort to allow everything, every place, and everyone to be exactly how it is at a given time. Essentially, it is living without trying to change, manipulate, or control things outside of oneself. Through trial and error (mostly error! Lol!), I have discovered that my life feels better when I surrender and get to a place of acceptance. I find myself able to be alright in a world that oftentimes is not so alright.

Joanne replies:

My first thought is, let go let God, and my second is acceptance is the answer to all my problems today. Just because I accept something doesn't mean I like it or I agree with it. It is what it is. I'm going to let it be. If it is detrimental to me in anyway, it doesn't have to be in my life. Stop chopping away at things that don't belong or are hurtful as long as I learned my lesson from it. Sometimes I push things away because they are too painful at that moment, and those things will keep coming back until I resolve them or accept them.

Upon reflecting on what others thought of surrender and acceptance, it got me thinking. Aras talks about being right or free. I like to add being right or happy. Has someone ever told you a story that you know is wrong? You realize that the information is not exactly right. For example, I gave my friend directions to my house, and she did not follow the directions and made a wrong turn. When she got to my house and informed me of this, I reviewed my directions and realized she turned too soon. So, at the time, I thought I had two choices, explain to her I gave the right directions and be right, or I could let go and have a nice visit with her. I choose the latter. Since being on this healing journey, I have come to understand that this is an "and" world. Meaning, there probably was a way for both of us to be right and happy. And my limiting beliefs and programming have prevented me from seeing other options. Tuesday talks about letting go of beliefs. What else am I not seeing that is available to me? What else are you not seeing that is available to you?

Surrendering and accepting are sometimes easy and sometimes hard and everything in between. There are days when I accept everything and days I accept nothing. When I am **NOT** in the accepting realm of reality, I ask, "What is the lesson here for me?" Then I say, "Please help me to see this sooner rather than later." After that, I need to be open to how the answer shows up. I can tell you it rarely shows up in the way I am expecting. Sometimes it is painful, and I must feel through the pain and get to the other side.

Here are some tools for surrendering.

Meditation - try it. It calms the mind. Yes, the mind wanders, and if you need more information on meditation and where to begin, I would like to suggest the book, Meditation for Fidgety Skeptics by Dan Harris and Jeff Warren.

Journaling – ask yourself why this is happening and keep asking until you get the answer. I journal one page a day on the subjects I am struggling with. Some days, the only thing written on my paper is the same question over and over again. Other days, the answer comes immediately. You can only do this right. Allow the answers to come when the time is right.

Speak out loud – whether that means talking to God or the Universe. Speak what you want to happen, and then allow it to happen.

Go out for a walk – being out in the air is grounding and helps the thought process.

Visualize – visualize where you want to go and release where you have been. The mind is powerful. Visualize and include as many of your senses as possible. What will it feel like when you have what you want? What will it look like? What will it sound like? What will it taste like? Transport yourself to your new reality and keep repeating this until you get there.

Forgive yourself with ease and grace – this gets easier over time. In the beginning, I used to berate myself and be so hard on myself when I made a mistake. I have come to understand that forgiving myself is part of self-love. Would you berate your friend for making a mistake? Or would you tell them it's really not a big deal? I find most of the time, I can forgive myself because it really is not a big deal.

During this journey of surrender that ultimately leads to acceptance of what is brought to me, I understand that I am creating my life. I create the good, and I create the bad. There are, of course, lessons in both, and we tend to learn more from our pain than our pleasure. Now, I am looking at the things that bring me joy and finding new ways to create more joy for myself. I am shifting my focus to the positive, and I am excited to see where this pivot will take me.

I have come to understand that surrender and acceptance have led me to certainty. I am confident I am on the correct path. I am certain that my life will continue to improve and I will become happier and more at peace with each passing day. This certainty opens up my mind to new opportunities that I may not previously have noticed when I was trying to control everything and ended up controlling nothing. What a peaceful place surrender and acceptance have become for me.

I would like to invite you to look at your life and what you have created. Are you content where you are or do you need to pivot? Discovering the joy of looking at the positive side of the situation has brought me a sense of peace and joy. It's my wish for you to be here with me.

"Progress instead of perfection." - Lisa Manzo

"Give yourself permission to be human, then forgive yourself." - Lisa Manzo

About the Author

Lisa Manzo has overcome depression and addiction and is now living a life of joy. Lisa is an author, speaker, emotional trauma coach, hypnotist, NLP master practitioner, teacher, and nurse who has extensive life experience working with clients and working to improve herself. Lisa had released the limiting beliefs that used to hold her back and is utilizing the tools that helped her to help others.

Lisa's natural intuition enables her to direct you through the process of becoming your true self. Lisa is fiercely committed to empowering people to open their minds to other available possibilities when they are looking.

To book a discovery call, email Lisa at:
Email: Lisa@ThePhoenixMind.com
Website: www.ThePhoenixMind.com

Hershey Ann Duenas, MBA

CHAPTER THREE

THE POWER OF BEING ALONE

At the age of 3, my parents left me at my grandparent's door because they couldn't take care of me, not because they don't want to but because they felt incapable. My mom got pregnant at the age of 16, and my dad was 18 at that time with a lack of maturity and different priorities. Growing up, I felt so different and uneasy, especially during my grade school years as I was always bullied. People said that my parents are old; meanwhile, they were talking about my grandparents and I was then called "adopted". At a very young age I felt alone, insecure, and unworthy. These feelings were carried into my teenage years until one day I looked at my grandparents and saw how much they loved me unconditionally and always present anytime I need them; that's the game-changer.

I became overly active and an achiever during my high school and college years because I feel the need to give back to my grandparents for believing in me and supporting me more than what parents can do. I was alone but never lonely because they got my back. Achievements and success became so addicting, especially when it brings smiles and tears of joy to the people that you love.

I became a parent when I was 22. Was I scared? Hell yes! But the first time I saw Tiara's face and held her in my arms, I immediately whispered in her ears "We got this baby."

I remember my grandmother asked me "now that you are a mother, what will you do now?" So I answered her back "Whatever it takes." Things didn't always go as planned, especially in relationships or marriage, and that's what happened to me. I became a single mom and had to do a reality check and wear two hats.

Again I felt alone...

I was sitting one-day drinking coffee when my grandmother talked to me and said, "Do what you know how to do best and I will support you." That made me realized that I wasn't alone. I was like, "Come on' I still have the best grandparents in the whole world." So I said I need to step up on my career in order to provide more, and she just smiled. I immediately recognized that kind of smile. A smile that means she knew I could make it and a smile that showed how proud she was, even when I wasn't there yet. I didn't plan to be a single parent, but I planned to be the best parent that I can be.

"Being a single parent is not a life full of struggles, but a journey for the strong."
~Meg Lovett

And so my journey began, I started working with Samsung Mobile, and seriously, it wasn't easy. Samsung at that time was not known for mobile phones but appliances. We were the pioneer who first introduced it to the market. Since I was all new in the industry, I managed the small accounts while the older employees were making tons of money handling bigger accounts and distributors. The funny thing about my assigned accounts was that they are either delinquent or lock in with other brands, meaning they are exclusively tied with the competitor. One day, my boss called me in and told me to meet with one of my clients who was the hardest to handle. No one in the office could really talk to her because she's loyal to the competitor and second she is just so hard to deal with. My boss suddenly compared me with the other sales who originally handled the client until she migrated to the US. I remember my boss telling me "Madz convinced and got her in for two weeks" so at least try your best to talk to her. I felt embarrassed and went on with my meeting and immediately reported back to the office. My boss called me in again for updates and said how did it go? Did you even talk? And so I answered and said "Madz convinced her in two weeks while I convinced and got her in for two hours." He couldn't believe it.

I believe that there will always be people who will belittle, doubt, and criticize you in every journey. I guess it's true what they say if someone mistreats you, just remember that it is a reflection of them, not you. Don't take everything personal. Let people be and focus on you and your growth. I learned that the hard way and the next thing you know I was one of the top sales in the office and guess what? Motorola pirated me to handle their house accounts. Boom!

In quite a few years I established my name in the Telecom industry in which they call it "A man's world." I became the National Sales Head of Lenovo Mobile at the age of 27 then got hired by Blackberry amongst the many veteran applicants in the industry. I also remember one of my junior sales asked me a question about how I did it. "How did you climb so fast to where you are right now in this industry?" I just smiled back and said, "I wasn't given a choice." That is true about life; sometimes it takes an overwhelming breakdown to have an undeniable breakthrough. And the plus side of going through the worst period in your life is knowing that rock bottom didn't kill you, but it made you stronger.

At the peak of my career, my grandmother had an accident and underwent surgery. She had her hip replacement down to her left knee. It was devastating because I hated seeing her in pain, lying in the hospital bed and not watching our favorite TV series at home. She has been in and out of the hospital for quite a while and then she passed away. I've never experienced pain like that. For me she wasn't just my grandmother, she was my mother, my best friend, my number one fan and now she became my angel. I think I'm going to grieve until it's my time.

"The reality is that you will grieve forever. You will not 'get over' the loss of a loved one; you will learn to live with it. You will heal and you will rebuild yourself around the loss you have suffered. You will be whole again but you will never be the same. Nor should you be the same or would you want to."

~ Elizabeth Kubler-Ross and David Kessler

The thing is, my grandmother taught me everything I knew about life. She was a chef, so she taught me how to cook. Since I was younger, she taught me how to basically be a woman, treat people right, and believe in myself but not how to say goodbye. So I struggled to live without her specially my daughter loved her too. Later that year, I was diagnosed with severe depression and anxiety. I had to be under medication or else I wouldn't function. I am so grateful that I had a good support system at that time. I was advised to take my medication for at least 1-2 years religiously until I decided to stop on the 6th month. Whoever experienced taking anti-depressants and anxiety pills would agree with me that it makes you feel more like a robot. I don't feel like myself and I don't have emotions at all. I went back to doing muay thai and working out at the gym religiously instead. I chose the healthier way. I guess whenever we face struggles and defeat, somehow we lose our sense of trying, but it's important to make it a habit of asking ourselves, "Does this support the life I'm trying to create?" If the answer is no then stand up, walk and stick to the plan.

Easier said than done? Yes. I'm guilty.

I flew to the US after three years to have a fresh start or should I say new beginnings. I read about this thing called "the fresh start" effect. According to the fresh start effect, people are more likely to take action towards a goal after a temporal landmark that represent new beginnings. Now, what is a temporal landmarks? It is a point in our time that we naturally think about the opportunity for a fresh start. This comes in two forms:

- **Social Temporal Landmarks** – Dates that are seen as a fresh start by many people collectively – New Year's, the start of a month, the start of a week, etc.
- **Personal Temporal Landmarks** – Dates that we personally see as a fresh start – birthdays, anniversaries, the start of a new job or semester, major moves or life changes.

As you can see, there are plenty of opportunities to get a fresh start, not just during New Year's. Mine just happened to be a major change in my life losing the mother I have known my whole life. According to Daniel Pink in his book When, it's because temporal landmarks allow us to open new "mental accounts." This will help us to focus on our goals and be able to be proactive in what changes will get us there.

I really believe temporal landmarks work in helping each person achieve their goals. When I relocated here to the US in late 2016, I immediately enrolled myself in the gym close to my house. I wasn't that consistent maybe because it's holiday season and it's cold (I wasn't used to cold weather) and it can get boring too. Come January, I saw new faces almost every week signing up for membership and posting this "new year, new me, who you" or "diet starts today" thing. I guess setting up new goals around a certain date is nothing new at all.

"When temporal landmarks psychologically disconnect us from our inferior, past self and make us feel superior, we will be motivated to behave better than we have in the past and strive with enhanced fervor to achieve our aspirations." ~Jeremy Anderberg

In two years, I got my real estate license. Honestly, it wasn't easy as this is a new industry for me coming from the tech world and I was close to giving birth. I was about seven months pregnant when I started to report to our brokerage office for orientation and trainings. Learning new things always amazes me. You see, temporal landmarks give you a new clean launching pad vibe that will take you in a brand-new direction. A breath of fresh air.

Speaking of a breath of fresh air, I welcomed my second baby girl – Tori. They said you can never experience the same love twice, but I did. I think some mothers will agree with me that once you loved your first born too much without expecting you will have another one, the second one becomes terrifying in the sense that you might show favoritism or how can the second one take some space in your heart when it is fully occupied by the first one. I was terrified. But then, the very moment I held Tori in my arms, I felt God gave me another heart that is just full of her. Then suddenly I got the same thought when I gave birth to my first born, "I need to step up with my career" now that I have two girls watching me.

I went back to business as fast as I could until it peaked, then COVID-19 showed up in the picture. Being consistently active in the business and trying to be safe is hard to weigh in. So I thought about being productive and achieving my goals considering lockdowns and quarantine that keep happening in the world right now. I don't want to be one of those people whose depression came back because they became helpless in these sad events. So I decided to take my MBA. Again, I thought it's going to be easy but it's not. Juggling school, work, house chores, and yes a newborn is not a good combination. I remember doing three thesis every week and everyday homework makes me want to puke at night. The earliest I can start with my school was like 9 PM (that's when I'm done with everything) to 2 AM and wakes up at 6 AM for the baby to feed. You can guess how many times I cried and thought of quitting school but I didn't. Why? Because there are still people rooting for me. I remember how my grandfather was so proud of me. Every time I shared new stories or even the course I have hard time understanding, he will just laugh at me and say, "Phew, you got this"! I am blessed to have a good support system even though they are far it seems they are just beside me. I think that that's the secret of overcoming anything, surrounding yourself with people who love you and people that make you believe in your power.

Let's talk about celebration. After two years of schooling, tadaaa! I graduated on my exact birthday last October 2020. I belong to the class of 2020. They call pandemic graduates. The sad part was commencement was canceled but the good news was, hey we made history! It's just how you look at life. Yeah, I mastered it.

When I saw my graduation photos hanging on the wall, I was in awe and still amazed by how much a person can accomplish if they won't stop until they get it. Life is only as good as your mindset. I become addicted to progress, and I fell in love with the process. I learned that slowing down is a beautiful thing, and patience may be bitter, but its fruit is sweet.

Speaking of bitterness, earlier this year, my grandfather became sick and couldn't eat. He got so much bacteria in his system that made him weak. He then passed away at 84.

Again, they said you would never experience the same pain twice, but I did. The only good thing was he's not in pain anymore and I got the chance to video call him to say I love you a lot of times. I was able to thank him for everything he has done. I got the chance to hear his I love you too's. I was able to tell him to rest well and look for my grandma and thank her for me.

The worst part is that I wasn't there. I am alone now. I felt like an orphan. As I've said earlier, they are considered my parents. Those are my cheerleaders. I am at the lowest of my life right now and breathing hurts. Knowing my grandfather, he doesn't want me to live like this. I heard from his nanny that he told her a few days before he died that he was so proud of me and wanted me to continue with what I'm doing. That breaks me and builds me up at the same time.

The best memory I had with him was when I got my first job at PLDT; he cried in front of me and said "You know I am so proud of you." He was the best father and grandfather for me. I just need to have a mindset that now I have two guardian angels watching my family and me.

"It's true what they say life doesn't get easier or more forgiving, you just get stronger. You learn to cope better, you become grateful amidst the chaos and hardships."
~Steve Maraboli

Life is full of uncertainty that's why anything is possible.

I didn't have a normal childhood as my grandparents raised me, and I don't have siblings. I learned the lesson at an early age that it doesn't matter what your parents did or did not do, but we must take full responsibility for our actions and choose to be a champ rather than to play a victim. Don't be bitter, be better. This is your story so write it the way you wanted.

People asked me what I will do now? I'm not going to lie, there were still nights I breakdown, nights that I couldn't sleep, nights that all I pray is asking why. I had to pick up the pieces and continue with my journey. I learned to rest and not to quit. Life can really be tough and demanding so slowing down is necessary to stay focus. I live by this bible verse that I actually tattooed on my rib cage *"You do not realize now what I am doing, but later you will understand" (John 13:7).* I always remind myself about this verse because I tend to really be impatient. I get jealous too when I see people having what I keep praying for. Until I talked with our pastor long way back, and he told me "God's delay is never God's denial." I think most of us are guilty of this. The best analogy I will have on this one is that when you order something special on the menu, be ready to wait; if not, then order in fast food. Special moments, people, or opportunities sometimes take a while to come but definitely it's worth the wait. But be ready when it comes!

You attract what you are ready for.

The power of manifestation and the law of attraction is factual. Whether it is opportunity or relationship, we attract what we are. The person who reminded me of this is my first born – Tiara. She is turning 16 this year so we talk like adults or should I say she talk me like an adult now (Jesus, how time flies!). I'd been stressed so she reminded me to think positive and think about what I want to attract, and it will happen.

I remember watching "the secret" and reading up on "the law of attraction" and "ask and it is given," they all talk about energy and vibration. When you send out a frequency, it will be reciprocated at the same rate. Like attracts like. Hate attracts hate.

Similarly, with relationships. When you learn to value yourself and never tolerate disrespect from anyone, you will also attract a person who share the same values and principles. Self-love isn't selfish; it's important. You have to love your own company, fall in love with your flaws, forgive yourself and commit to your progress. Truly love yourself, and you know why? You cannot give what you do not have. Imagine getting into a serious relationship before you are even ready to handle it. This is how we waste time and our energy. However, once we are fully ready then right things, right people will come at the right time.

You cannot love others unless you love yourself first.

"Attract what you expect, reflect what you desire,
become what you respect, mirror what you admire."
~Unknown

The universe will keep giving you the same lessons, same relationships, same pain, same wrong love until it will force you to realize that the common denominator is you. The thing is, the universe can be tricky sometimes. You have to shout at the top of your lungs the things you want to attract simply because the universe wants you to want it bad enough.

It happened to me many times when I wanted it so bad, it will definitely be given to you. But then again, you have to work for it. The job, the dream, and relationship it all need hard work.

So, I challenge you all today to think and manifest whatever you want to attract or change in your life and do the next right thing. Let God work behind the scenes and let the universe work on your behalf to give you what you are ready for.

Keep the faith!

"For I know the plans I have for you,' declares the Lord, 'plans to prosper you and not to harm you, plans to give you hope and a future."
~ (Jeremiah 29:11)

About the Author

Hershey Ann Duenas was born in the Philippines and relocated to Southern California in 2016. Before obtaining her real estate license in 2017, she spent 15 years in leadership & sales within the telecom and advertising industry.

Hershey is a member of the Pacific West Association of REALTORS®, California Association of REALTORS®, National Association of REALTORS®, and Certified Short Sale and Foreclosure Resource Specialist. She is now a Co-Owner of Intellivest Realty to cater all service real estate across California.

Hershey holds a Masters Degree in Business Administration at Grand Canyon University and a Certification in Contract Law at Harvard University.

To collaborate and learn more about Hershey:
Website: www.goaskhershey.com
Email: hbduenas@gmail.com
LinkedIn: https://www.linkedin.com/in/hersheybautista/
IG: https://www.instagram.com/realtorhershey

Sarah Ferguson
BMus/BEd, MEd, AMusA

CHAPTER FOUR

THE CHOICE OF TRANSFORMATION

Transformation means different things to different people. To some, it seems like this intangible, abstract concept that people wait to have happened but never really know if it has. They assume that if they think about it enough, one day, they will magically feel different. For others, they believe if they go to enough conferences, repeat the right affirmations, and change their mindset, everything will fall into place. What people often forget is that transformation comes from thousands of choices we make daily. It's not something that magically appears. It's not something that someone else can do for you. It's hard work, and it is a choice. Yes, you need to be open to change, open to seeking opportunities for growth and be reflective. But does that mean you have to drip with positivity, superficial platitudes, and affirmations twenty-four hours a day, seven days a week? No.

Twenty years ago, I had the world at my fingertips. I grew up in regional Australia, moved away from everything I knew when I turned eighteen to the 'big smoke' to follow my dream to study music. After this, I moved to England to continue my pursuit of happiness. By 2008, I was living and working in London and had my entire future in front of me, and it was bright. From a young age, I knew I wanted to pursue music. I worked hard, made sacrifices, embraced every opportunity that came my way, endured emotional abuse from my violin teacher at university, and persevered through the competitive world of music. I practiced long and hard hours to achieve my goals. I was determined to prove wrong every person that said, "You can't make it as a musician; that's just an unrealistic childish dream." I had a plan, and I was going to make it happen.

After my time in England, I was back in Australia and staying with family while interviewing for jobs across Australia. It was the 18th of August 2010 at about 4 p.m. I was driving to meet my sister at my family home. Suddenly, a truck pulled out of a side street in front of me. In one second, one mistake was made by one stranger. Life changed forever.

A lady in the car behind me pulled over to talk to me while I waited for the ambulance to arrive. I couldn't move, couldn't see, and certainly wasn't game to try. The lady that started talking to me was a nurse at the local hospital. She called the paramedics to give them a heads up of what to expect and to check if there was anything she could do to help in the meantime. They were on loudspeaker and asked if she could see any bleeding. She indicated that I was bleeding from my nose. They asked her to just squeeze my nose to try and stop the bleeding until they arrived. Hesitantly, she replied, "Look, you'll understand why that is not possible when you get here." Little did they know that my nose was in my eye socket. I took a deep breath. At that point, I knew that this would not be a quick and simple recovery.

The next few days were a blur. Emergency surgeries, consultations with local specialists, coming in and out of consciousness. Local surgeons came to have a look and very quickly let us know these surgeries were out of their league and I would need to travel to Brisbane. I wasn't surprised. But what came next was mortifying. The doctor in charge of my case told my family, "Don't worry, if they aren't willing to operate, we'll find someone in town willing to give it a go." My heart sunk; my families' hearts sunk. I grabbed my sister's hand, told her to get my phone and call one of my dearest friends from my college days. His dad was a doctor in a small country town, but I knew without a doubt I could trust that they would do everything they could to help. In a matter of days, he had organized for the Royal Flying Doctors Service to fly me to Brisbane and referred me to the best Maxillofacial Surgeon and Orthopaedic Surgeon in Queensland.

I was flown to Brisbane late one night and was transported to the hospital, which would become my home for the near future. That night was the first time I hadn't had someone with me. My family couldn't come on the flight, and it was a very long drive to the city. It was dark, it was quiet, and I was afraid. I didn't know yet, what my new surgeons would say. I didn't know if I would see again, walk again, or play the violin again. There is nothing quite like the deafening silence of uncertainty and the debilitating fear that comes with no longer having any control over what would happen next. I was a planner, a mover, and a shaker. I was a fiercely independent human, and I made things happen. I soon learned the insecurity that comes with no longer being in control and the excruciating vulnerability of having to trust and rely on others.

The coming weeks were filled with grueling surgeries and painful, sleepless nights. Through all of this, my parents and sisters were incredible. I knew without a doubt that they were there fighting the good fight 24 hours a day, making sure I was never physically alone. For this, I will be eternally grateful. At the same time, I knew that they were also going through hell and back. I knew in my head that whatever happened, it was going to be ok. I didn't really know that, but I was determined to make it true even if it wasn't true. They didn't know this, and I couldn't communicate it with them. They could see the damage; they knew the full extent of my injuries. My parents have both worked in the health industry. They weren't naïve to the reality. I can't even begin to imagine the fear that my parents were feeling. I can't even imagine the weight on my sisters' shoulders as they were trying to support my parents, support me, and keep their own personal lives together. And there was nothing I could do to help, nothing I could do to support them.

My first major surgery and the start of my journey back to my new normal was maxillofacial. The simplest way I can explain this type of surgery is when a surgeon rebuilds your facial structure using titanium plates. The steering wheel had crushed a very distinctive section of my face. As a result, they had to remove whatever bone fragments they could and replaced these sections with titanium plates and, in the case of my eye socket, titanium mesh. My family was told the procedure would take about 4 hours. It ended up taking nearly double the amount of time. My incredibly talented surgeon was happy with how everything went and was incredibly reassuring to my family and I. I still remember one of my follow-up appointments about a year after all my initial surgeries. My doctor was as proud as punch of the work that he did. He had a special folder on his computer where he kept records of his most unusual cases. It may seem strange but being in that folder felt like it was a badge of honor. Like I was a part of some special group of people that took incredible skill and imagination to help

My second major surgery was on my wrist. This was the one that I was most concerned about. The success of this surgery determined whether I would be able to play the violin again. My orthopedic surgeon originally indicated that this would not be possible. I was not particularly happy with this response and apparently indicated that he needed to do his job better. I blame my impertinence on the extreme painkillers I was on at the time. But in hindsight, I am grateful I got my point across. Two surgeries later, and close to twelve months of hand therapy and I can play again. Not to the same standard, and not without pain, but I can play. Let's be honest, taking the good with the bad is a part of life.

Due to a rather grueling recovery, my family restricted visitors as much as they could. When I did receive them, I would always try to put on a happy face and give it my all to pretend everything was ok. Although in saying that, I couldn't move my mouth or open my eyes, so 'happy face' may be the wrong choice of words. Let's go with 'inside happy face.' As a result, I would always be exhausted for the few days following. I know that having people in your life that want to visit and make sure you are ok is wonderful. However, during this time of my life, it was also terrifying. There were two visits that have always stayed with me. The first knew that I had been hurt in an accident but didn't really know what had happened. She came in so excited to see me, but by the time she had reached my bedside her voice had softened, and her hands were shaking. We tried to have a normal conversation as if nothing were wrong, but under the circumstances, that wasn't the easiest thing to do. When we reminisce about it now, she always insists that she knew the experience hadn't changed me because I spent the whole time making sure she was ok. The second visitor was the friend that my family had called asking for his father's help. He is one of the kindest, strongest, and steadfast people I have ever had the privilege of calling a friend. I hoped that as he had spoken to his father, he would have arrived knowing what to expect. However, even he was trembling as he held my hand. You never really know what is going on in someone's mind, but it felt like he was afraid that if he squeezed my hand too hard, I would crumble. He didn't know what to say at the time, and neither did I. We just existed for a short while hoping everything would turn out ok. It was gut wrenching. Neither of us knew if anything would ever be the same again.

Eight weeks on and I was discharged from the hospital. Still quite fragile both physically and emotionally, but determined that everything would be ok. I had to stay in Brisbane for a few weeks just in case anything went wrong. However, I soon got to travel back home to the comfort of my own bed. My knee was still unstable. I had what we affectionately termed 'bootie' on my right foot and a cast on my wrist and face. The following weeks were celebrating milestone after milestone. I was showering on my own, toileting on my own, being able to focus on something and no longer see in double, cutting up shallots, standing up on my own, increasing the range of motion in my wrist by 1 millimeter at a time. It was hard but also satisfying. I began to see a light at the end of the tunnel. What I didn't expect was my next curveball.

It was a Wednesday, and I had a check-up with my maxillofacial surgeon. Dad and I traveled down in the morning. I was a bit excited. It was the day they were going to take the last fifty staples out of my head and hopefully remove the last piece of my face cast. My doctor and I were having a good yarn, and he was sharing some of his memories from my time in hospital. He then took the remaining piece of cast off my face and held up a mirror so I could see myself for the first time since the accident. I turned to him and asked if I would look like me again when all the swelling went down. He just looked at me shocked and indicated that the swelling had gone down, then asked, "Is that not what you looked like beforehand?" I simply replied, "No." I hadn't really thought about what I would look like yet. I know that sounds strange; I had a steering wheel smash through my face. You would probably think that would be on my mind. I don't know whether it was because I was so focused on my wrist or focused on walking and seeing again. I'm not sure. My dad could see I was freaking out and took over the conversation for a bit. I soon held it together for long enough to start making conversation again. He indicated that if I wanted to, I could see a plastic surgeon to get their opinion on what they could do. However, he wanted me to be aware that any procedure could be unpredictable and risky with the amount of scar tissue that had developed. I smiled and thanked him for everything. He had, after all, genuinely done an amazing job. But at that moment, I needed to get out as fast as I could. Dad and I got into the elevator and went down to the car. I burst out into tears.

Dad quickly called the family to let them know what had happened. I never considered myself a particularly vain person. I always had a relatively good level of self-esteem. But this really threw me. I had lost so much; I had fought to get so much back. This was something that no amount of anything could change. I couldn't therapy my way out of changing my facial structure. I couldn't change my face by changing my mindset. It wasn't set in stone but was set by titanium. I knew that plastic surgery could do more damage than good. I had a four-hour drive home. I cried for a good three hours. Then suddenly, I just stopped. After a few minutes, dad asked me if I needed to talk. I looked at him and said, "I just have to accept it, don't I?" He sighed and responded with, "Well, we can go and see any plastic surgeon you want, but yes, there is a very good chance that you will just have to accept it." At that moment, I had to make a choice.

Would I let this get the better of me? After everything that had happened, this was not going to be my undoing. Whether I wanted it to or not, this was what I looked like now. By the time I got home, my family had made all my favorite foods. There was Curried Chicken, Continental Choc Chip Cheesecake, Clinkers, and Fantales. You name it, it was there. My mother and sisters tiptoed around the subject for a while. But no amount of talking about it was going to change anything. There was no point wallowing in self-pity. I had made my choice, and it was time to get on with things.

Don't get me wrong, there have been some excruciatingly hard moments since. The first time I caught up with one of my closest friends after the accident, he just hugged me and whispered in my ear, "Still just as beautiful as ever." I won't lie, I cried that night. One year, I was supposed to go to my College's 100th Anniversary Ball. At the time, I couldn't bear to spend the evening potentially having to introduce myself to people that knew me well, purely because they didn't recognize me. I had made my choice, but it didn't mean it wasn't hard to live with the realities of it. Some mornings when I wake up extremely tired, I will scare the living daylights out of myself when I look in the mirror, and for a split second, I don't recognize the person in front of me. But on these days, just like every other day, I must make a choice.

In so many ways, I am still the vibrant, energetic, determined person I have always been. So many friends will comment that I may look different, but I am still the same quirky, fun-loving person on the inside. However, there is something that has transformed. I now know that nothing is certain, and that's ok. I can't control everything, but I can control how I respond to the uncontrollable. That perfection doesn't exist. It is like the horizon; it recedes as you approach it. A career does not make you happy, nor does money, fame, or success. What makes you happy is what goes on inside your mind. And that is a choice that you make every day. When you make a mistake, you have the choice to give yourself a hard time about it and give up or take responsibility for it, learn from it, and move on. You have the option to let your past control you or learn from your past and grow.

The accident could have been the very worst thing that happened to me. I could be miserable about no longer being able to perform like I used to. I could refuse to have music in my life because it reminds me of what I lost. I could be too ashamed to walk outside my house because I didn't want to accept and embrace my new face. But instead, the accident has been the best thing that ever happened to me. I now value life more than I ever thought I could. Every day, I see the value of my loving family, the incredible people in my life, and the ability to help others through my work. But most of all, I know that every day I have a choice to maintain the transformation that has happened to me over the past ten years. And that is the most rewarding choice I will ever make.

About the Author

Sarah Ferguson has 15 years of experience as a teacher, musician, and leader. Her unique background has driven her to help others to develop resilience, a positive sense of self and determination to live their best lives. She has first-hand experience working with children and adults to develop both their personal and professional lives. Sarah is acutely aware of the challenges that people face in life and is passionate about helping others to develop strategies to make the most out of everything that comes their way.

LinkedIn: https://www.linkedin.com/in/sarah-ferguson85
Email: sarahferguson85@gmail.com

Ann Wood

CHAPTER FIVE

MY LEADERSHIP JOURNEY

It was a beautiful Monday morning in early Spring. The sun was shining, the birds were chirping, and a crisp breeze caressed my skin as I walked towards the office. I felt on top of the world. I felt so energized, excited, and privileged that I was in a job where I could support children, youth, and families in vulnerable, abusive, and often dangerous situations to find happiness, hope, and feel safe again knowing their future looks bright.

As I sat down at my desk, turned my computer on, and was getting ready for the day it was refreshing to hear all the laughter and chatter around the office. Everyone was sharing stories of what they did over the weekend, creating an atmosphere and energy in the office that was so positive, inspiring, and uplifting.

As the clock struck 9 am, my phone started ringing, emails quickly filled my inbox, and people arrived at reception for scheduled meetings. My day was off to a great and busy start with the usually 'unexpected' problems arising left, right, and center. I enjoyed the rush of doing what I love. I quickly became very good at creatively solving problems, adapting to new situations, and juggling numerous balls in the air to help support others. Life was great.

Before I knew it, I had written ten emails, spoken to eight people on the phone, signed off on two reports, and had two successful face-to-face meetings. The morning had flown by so quickly as it was already time for morning tea, despite the usual ups and downs, which is the nature of the work. I was in a role where I was responsible for supporting people experiencing domestic and family violence, disabilities, abuse, neglect, mental health issues, substance abuse, and homelessness, just to name a few. I was so passionate about supporting children, youth, adults, and families through some of the darkest times in their life. It was nice knowing my clients knew they could reach out and trust me with some of their deepest secrets.

I heard the main door close and very distinct footsteps walking along the corridor. My heart instantly sank into my stomach as I immediately recognized those footsteps. They were getting closer and closer. I could now feel the vibration of the steps on the floor as they continued straight past the area where I was sitting. The footsteps stopped once she entered her office. The energy in the office had immediately changed. The happy, jovial, and relaxed atmosphere had rapidly disappeared, and the office was now filled with negativity, toxic energy, and anxiety. You could have cut the tension with a knife. Once she had entered her office, we all looked around at each other in disbelief. We couldn't believe it. What was she doing here? Why is she in the office? She was supposed to be out of town at a conference. We thought we were going to have a wonderful three days. Apparently not.

This woman who so very powerfully and quickly changed the dynamic in the office was my manager, Shelley McTaggart. The woman who I report to. The woman I was supposed to feel comfortable with. The woman whose role, theoretically, is to provide a safe and supportive space for me to learn and grow. The woman who was to inspire, motivate, and empower me. The reality couldn't have been further from these responsibilities.

A few minutes later, Shelley exited her office and approached our team as we sat so very quietly at our desks diligently working. Shelley proceeded to very proudly announce that last week, due to unforeseen circumstances, the conference had been postponed. However, she chose not to tell us so she could surprise us. "Ta dah, I'm here," Shelley so proudly declared. Aren't we 'lucky? Everyone on the team was frightened of her. Once Shelley finished proudly announcing her presence, we quickly turned around to face our computers again while giving each other sideways glances of disappointment and hoping she didn't see us.

Shelley's behavior was rude, obnoxious, and arrogant. She always sought opportunities to exert her power as she got significance from intimidating others and made them feel frightened, incompetent, and inferior. Shelley micromanaged her team, except for Rebecca, of course. Essentially, Shelley's behaviors were that of the type of behaviors we supported our clients to change.

As part of our role and working in the industry, everyone was required to participate in supervision, a private monthly 1:1 meeting with your manager. The purpose of supervision is to provide individualized support and coaching to ensure quality practice, identify areas for growth as well as training and/or strategies for further development, recognize areas you are performing well, career development opportunities, and guidance for any other areas your or your manager ascertains to add value to your role. Shelley instead used this as an opportunity to go through everyone's work with a fine-tooth comb to identify fault and failure. I dreaded it; we all did. Every time I walked towards her office, I felt my body go into fight, flight, or freeze mode, and I hadn't even entered her office yet. I was fighting back tears within minutes.

I remember this one afternoon when myself and two colleagues all reached a breaking point. The pressure was too much to handle. We hid in one of the spare rooms out the back. We were all sitting in the corner, on the floor, with our heads in our hands, crying. It was too much. The way Shelley spoke to us and treated us was so rude and demeaning. Shelley was a bully. If I came to work early and left late, it wasn't good enough. If I was up to date with all my work, it wasn't good enough. If I received amazing feedback from a client or stakeholder, it wasn't good enough. Nothing I ever did seemed to satisfy Shelley enough to get off my back and stop being horrible to me.

I experienced this for many years, and as a result, it started to affect my health. I suffered from headaches, ulcers, tonsilitis, anxiety, depression, nightmares, as well as severe flu that would leave me bedridden for at least one week at a time. This was the only time I had a break from the toxic behavior. I was too scared to ever use one of my mental health days because Shelley would question me about why I 'chucked a sickie.' It just wasn't worth it.

Throughout the years of working under Shelley, she would often brag that previous staff in her teams have tried to take her for bullying in the past. Shelley would always laugh about it and then brag about how she always got off the allegations. She would always finish those conversations with 'if any of you try, good luck because it won't work, as I will get off any of your allegations too.'

After working in these conditions for years, my friends (and colleagues) laughed and joked as they nicknamed me 'Angry Ann' because my personality had changed so much from when I first started working in this sector. I was now always so stressed, unhappy, and lacked patience, which was different from the Ann when I first started. This was a huge 'light bulb' moment for me as it helped me see I didn't deserve to be treated like that. Something had to change, and it had to happen fast. I wanted to return to being my true self, which was happy, fun, and vivacious. I immediately started looking for other positions.

A few months later, I was presented with another opportunity that looked interesting, so I applied. A few weeks later, I was invited to participate in an interview, and soon after, I received a phone call to say I was the successful applicant and when can I start. I was thrilled. I finally had the chance to escape from these toxic working conditions. I believed that nowhere could be as bad as what I had experienced. I wrote my letter of resignation. I had mixed emotions about telling my manager as I was so excited I was finally going to leave, but at the same time, I was scared of her reaction and rightly so, as she made the following two weeks hell. Shelley upped her anti, her behavior worsened, and she kept changing the goal post as to the expected quantity of work I needed to complete before my last day. I still don't know how I made it through.

I started my new job, and it was great. New people, new environment, new clients, new tasks to challenge me and help me grow, different ways to help others and a fresh start. I was so optimistic. I had such high hopes. Only to be let down, yet again as the honeymoon phase of this job lasted just as long as it did at my last workplace, not very long. I soon saw through the cracks and tried to fill the gaps, only to learn that this management team also similarly conducted themselves to the last workplace. I lost hope very quickly. Day after day, I asked myself, "What's the point of trying? Why isn't management open to new ideas? How is it they can't see what they are doing isn't working?" If it wasn't for my strong desire to help others, I would have given up.

I felt my mood change each weekday morning when I realized I needed to start getting ready for work. I felt this heaviness in the pit of my stomach, the muscles in my neck tightened, and some days, I almost felt like I would be sick. Over the years, I started being more conscious of the physiological changes in my body between when I felt great and was having fun compared to when I was either at work, needed to speak to my boss, or even just thought about going into the office. It amazed me as I noticed that pretty much the whole time when I was at work, I was 'on edge.' I felt nervous, anxious, targeted, and vulnerable whilst also feeling invisible, unimportant, and worthless. I knew that even when I did make a suggestion that just might improve something, I knew I would be ignored, laughed at, or appeased.

After years of working in the industry, I had many similar experiences with numerous different supervisors, managers, leadership teams, and organisations. Some leaders are aware of their destructive conduct and authoritarian approach, while others are ignorant to their demeaning soul destroying behaviour. Both of which result in toxic workplace culture and poor organisational performance. I noticed that most teams and organizations were all characterized with similar attitudes, qualities, and practices, including lack of flexibility, not open to change, poor staff morale, mediocre performance, lack of clear direction, not valuing the efforts of the team and not addressing the underlaying issues, to name a few. These experiences only fuelled the fire in my soul to one day be the change I wanted to see in the world. I never understood why management teams weren't respectful, empathic, and transparent especially considering the environment and sector we all worked which is all about supporting, motivating, and empowering others. Why don't the management teams lead by example? Why isn't management being the change that is so desperately needed in this world? Why are they such control freaks, closed-minded, and self-centered? Why aren't the leadership teams willing to address the real issues to create a supportive work environment with a healthy culture where staff feel safe? If management actually addressed the cause of the problems, their teams would perform better, making them look better. Isn't that what they want?

This realization helped me to set a goal. I promised myself that I will climb the corporate ladder and be the leader I always wished I had. I will be the change I wanted to see in the world. I will be the leader that others aspire to be like. I will be the leader who shines the light. I will be the leader to raise the bar. I will be the leader to lead with certainty. I will be the leader who leads with clarity, self-awareness, emotional intelligence, flexibility, transparency, empathy, values my team, seeks to understand, communicates effectively, listens, creatively solve problems, embraces change, and has fun along the way.

To be a great leader, the type of leader I wanted to be, I knew I needed to further build on the knowledge I learnt through my formal university qualification Bachelor Science majoring in Psychology, and the invaluable practical experience I gained throughout my career. I spent many more hours studying, researching, and gaining further qualifications in related areas. The subjects include Leadership; Psychological Safety; Neuro capability; Neuro development; Quantum physics; Change management; Neuro Linguistic Programming; Success; Communication; Organisational Development; Mindset; as well as Executive & Life Coaching.

Over the next few years, I successfully climbed the corporate ladder to different leadership and executive roles. Finally, I was able to significantly impact the quality of leadership, organizational culture, and level of performance within my team, department, and organization. Rising to this position definitely wasn't an easy journey as it was confronting and hard work. I needed to be very honest with myself, listen to my body when I was triggered by others and remain focused on the bigger picture to ensure I committed 100% to overcoming the past experiences to create a new future, not only for myself but also for the rest of the workforce in this sector. No one deserves to be treated how I was. I used my experiences to stay motivated and follow my passion to make changes, lead the way and shine the light for those following my footsteps.

Being a leader isn't easy. I was often the odd one out as I looked at situations in a different light. I applied what I had learned as well as trialled new approaches to achieve better outcomes. I ensured everyone felt safe to contribute their ideas; felt safe in their environment; and felt safe to challenge practices or decisions allowing for innovation. I confidently and comfortably managed conflict; enjoyed creatively solving problems; shared in celebrating my team's success; and implemented a coaching approach to leading my team. I made timely decisions with excellence in mind (not perfectionism). I took decisive and deliberate action that was different from the status quo, knowing I was free to adapt, modify, and tweak things along the way. As a result, clients achieved better outcomes, my teams' individual, and group performance elevated, and the organization reached greater success. Win, win, win.

Over the years, I have had countless opportunities for further learning and development as I see failure as an opportunity for growth. I learned from my mistakes and the mistakes of others. I watched with a keen eye as to how other leaders achieve success. I listened to what other trailblazers say about their experiences. I observed others' behaviors. I knew that if I wanted to be the best version of myself, I needed to let my past experiences go and give myself permission to step into my greatness and lead with clarity, inspiration, passion, and integrity.

My leadership journey was born from a place of frustration and feeling powerless. My personal experience with my teams and through observation of other workplaces tell me this isn't something I was alone in feeling. Instead of resigning myself to a life of feeling frustrated and powerless, I turned the situation around and started thinking differently. What helped my colleagues and I do our jobs well? And what hindered us? Most importantly, why is my role important. The answers to these questions helped me to begin forming my ideas of leadership. They forged a way forward to create a more effective space to help the children, adults, and families in the community as well as the members of my team, department, and organization.

I am privileged to have raised the bar and become an industry leader in my field, as evidenced by the fact that years after leaving my position, organizations and service providers throughout multiple regions are now required to enhance their level of quality practice, innovative approaches to facilitate change and service delivery to meet the standard I set. Over the years, I was asked to participate in numerous consultative forums, collaborate on community projects, and advise community partners and stakeholders. The teams, community partners, and industry stakeholders I collaborated with and led over the years has taught me so many invaluable lessons which have supported my growth and development as an individual and professional. The amazing feedback I received continues to motivate and inspire me on my leadership journey. I feel very blessed to have had such a positive impact on those around me.

Over the last two decades, I have personally learned that to be a respected leader, it is essential to establish genuine connections and create a psychologically safe space. A few attributes that significantly enhanced my success include: seeking to understand; listen; remain curious; embrace change; effective communication; demonstrate clarity; display transparency, accountability, and integrity; be proactive; relish collaboration; ensure quality and timely decision making; practice emotional intelligence; value your team and acknowledge their efforts; and celebrate wins. I know these will also support you on your leadership journey too.

Leadership starts with me. Leadership starts with you. Leadership drives culture, culture drives performance. You can lead from where you are now, regardless of your title. Be the change you want to see in the world. Shine your light. Enjoy the journey. It starts with you. What choice do you make?

About the Author

Ann Wood is the founder and CEO of Ann Wood International. Ann is a trainer, consultant, speaker, and coach specialising in the Social Services Sector. Ann works with ambitious leaders, executives, and corporate teams improve their leadership, organisational culture, change management and performance to become industry leaders. During the last 20 years in the sector, she rose through the corporate ladder, to executive positions, overcoming adversity, and harnessing the invaluable knowledge, experience, insights, and wisdom which led her to creating her signature methodology. This methodology is what she implemented to create her own success. Ann now shares her exclusive methodology with high performing professionals and teams, to take their leadership to the next level.

Website: www.annwoodinternational.com
LinkedIn:
https://www.linkedin.com/company/ann-wood-international
Facebook:
https://www.facebook.com/Ann-Wood-International-101395128812325

Kyle,
Brother I appreciate the love & support as I embark on this new adventure! I want to be able to help others see the light they have to become the best version of themselves! I still have & cherish your score card framed in my office! You're an amazing person & honored to have met you! There was a reason behind it. Thanks & Be on the Lookout for more books to come!
Sean Steiner AKA The WizdKid

Sean Steiner

CHAPTER SIX

LETTING MY LIGHT SHINE

I grew up in a small Midwest town outside of Madison, WI, and was the youngest with two older brothers. My parents divorced and remarried at a young age. Growing up, I was a multiple-sport athlete varying from soccer, football, baseball, and basketball. As one could imagine, being the youngest and the smallest, I got picked on quite a bit growing up. Despite the constant heckling from my brothers and some of the neighborhood kids, I just wanted to be liked and fit in.

This led me to try marijuana with my older brother, Aaron,

at the young age of 12 and getting drunk on my 13th birthday. I still remember my mom catching me high for the first time, and I told her someone kicked dirt in my eyes. I don't know why I thought that was a good excuse, but what can I say? I took a shot. At about the same time, I tried smoking cigarettes and became an active smoker, which I continued till high school. By this time, all sports went out through the door because I wasn't willing to put in the work to get better. And it seemed easier not to try at all than to try and fail. I think the turning point for me was wanting to practice with the JV football team and was told by the coach I wasn't good enough to practice with them. He didn't give me any playing time. Mind you, I was really good at sports growing up and had natural talent but did not want to put in the work to continue performing at a higher level of competition. This led to me getting into trouble quite often between skipping class and getting kicked out of class for being the "funny guy." I was disrespectful to the teachers and students by constantly interrupting class, and not taking my studies seriously. This had gotten to a point where I was on the path of not going to be able to graduate on time. My mom had kicked me out of the house and lived at a friend's in a nearby town. I now realize that this was a cry for help. I wanted to do anything to get the attention due to my oldest brother Justin being excellent in academics and a multiple sport athlete. My other brother Aaron was outstanding in sports and a bit of a charmer with the ladies. I felt like I did not belong anywhere and as if I wasn't getting recognition by anyone, so I labeled myself the family's black sheep and ran with it. Since taking the approach of living "carefree" and not thinking of my future, I had stumbled onto a drug that made me feel good about myself, Vicodin. I was also experimenting with cocaine, was a habitual marijuana user, and went to any party that involved drinking.

By the summer going into my senior year, I had made it abundantly clear through my actions that I was not going to do anything to benefit myself, and so my mom and stepfather decided to send me to a wilderness therapy program in St. George, Utah. In this program, we were out in the desert elements for no set period. It was only when you complete the multiple chapters that you will graduate from the program. To set the tone of showing me a glimpse into what my future would hold if I continued this path, I was stripped and searched upon entering the program. My urine test came back positive for cocaine and marijuana. I was treated like an intake. No joke, I had to get completely naked, squat, and do a 360-degree turn. I was not comfortable because it was very cold in the intake room. However, I acquired an array of valuable skills varying from starting a fire with a shoestring that was tied to a thick branch for the bow, a rock, another stick, and a block of wood, to being able to make a knife from a piece of wood, a sharp rock, and making "poo glue" made with rabbit feces and tree sap. Basically, we learned everything you would in boy scouts. However, we were in the elements hiking every day, climbing mountains, eating dehydrated foods, showering with water bladders hung from a tree, making a campsite with a tarp and some strings, and more. At the moment, I was furious at my parents for sending me away, but now I realize that they were trying everything they could to help me, and it made me a stronger individual because of the experience. I thought all the fun was over, but I was wrong again.

After spending July through October in the great outdoors, I still had a lot of ground to cover in making up for all the credits that I was behind to graduate on time. However, they told me before I left the program that I was going right into boarding school, and there were no open negotiations at this point, so I had to play along because I was still seventeen. I was heartbroken because I missed my friends and family and wanted to get back to what I considered normalcy. The three of us took a road trip to reconnect and visit the boarding school I was to attend within a week. The boarding school was Discovery Academy that was located in Provo, Utah. At this point, I was about six to seven credits behind, and this was in October of my senior year. Fortunately for me, I had a counselor at my previous high school who really advocated for me to transfer my credits to my old school and graduate with my class after meeting the requirements. In the first two months in the school, I did minimal work and tried to find any excuse for my parents to bring me back home. Luckily, they did not budge and were insistent I finish my credits before I could come home.

Around Christmas time, I was allowed to come back home and visit with family and friends. I took this opportunity to make the most of my time to meet with some old friends to smoke weed, and at the time, spice (synthetic marijuana) was trending. The first couple of days, I did that and took niacin the last couple of days to get the stuff out in my system as my urine would be tested upon returning to the school. Now that I knew they were not going to budge, this was that moment I made a goal to get all of my credits by April 20th so that I could be back in time for my brother Aaron's birthday. This was a hint to myself that I could do anything I set my mind to. I worked tirelessly to achieve this goal I had set for myself, and at one point, developed anxiety attacks as a result of this. The staff was only able to count single-handedly the number of students who could accomplish that many credits within a four-month span due to my lack of effort in the first two months.

Nonetheless, I was on a flight home on April 20th, 2007, and had already intended to indulge in the well-recognized holiday. When I got home and saw my brother, he was excited to see me, but the excitement was short-lived. Little to my knowledge, he had already arranged some plans of his own with the girl he was seeing then, and I was devastated! We had been through a lot together, and I looked up to him as my hero. I mean, I worked my tail off only to be pushed to the side and learned another valuable lesson that day. Never expect people to give you the same efforts as you do, or you will be disappointed every time. Instead of spending the day with my brother, I went to my school to surprise my friends as I had the number of credits necessary to graduate. The looks I received were humorous. It was as if everyone had seen a ghost, and I am certain several rumors were circulated in my absence. Fast forward to my birthday on June 7th of 2007, I walked with my class and, of course, had indulged in some Mary Jane before the ceremony.

This next part is when things got really dark for my family and me. In the fall of 2007, my brother Aaron had gotten into trouble fighting and was in jail for a few months. After he had gotten out, he was out with some friends when he got into another fight, which meant an even longer jail sentence if he got caught. Somehow, the police officers found out he was involved in a fight and was looking at some major time. Then, I got a call from Aaron. He was very insistent on us going out to our dad's house ASAP, which was odd to me because it was so urgent. Of course, I met him there. While my dad and stepmom were cooking dinner, Aaron and I went and took a nap. Our dad called down to us that dinner was ready, so I had gone up to eat and Aaron never came up. We just figured he was just tired, so we put away some food so that he could get leftovers when he woke up. Later, my dad went to check in on him and was surprised where he found Aaron. He was in the back room with the lights off, staring up at the ceiling and not responding to anything we were saying. After a minute or so, he got up without saying a word. My dad yelled at him, but he acted as if he didn't see anyone and silently grabbed his keys and proceeded to leave. My dad is a big guy, but Aaron literally walked through my dad, got in his car, and drove away. My dad and I were in the doorway arguing about what the hell was going on, and I had no explanation for him.

I could only assume he was hallucinating. Little did we know that would be the last time we saw my brother alive. The next morning, my dad called me to tell me a sheriff's officer was doing his rounds on the back roads when he found Aaron on the side of the road. He had been rushed to the ER, and I immediately left to see him in the hospital. At this point, we found out from the doctors he had ingested antifreeze, and after doing many blood transfusions, his organs were shutting down. The only thing keeping him alive was the machines, and he would never have a quality life, so my parents had to make the tough decision of letting him rest in peace on October 31st, 2007. At this point, a piece of me died along with him. I became numb. I was not ready to lose my brother who I had seen as my hero and couldn't bear the fact of seeing him like that on the hospital bed.

This was the point where I did anything I could to

drown out the pain of losing my brother, living by the code 'that there is no guarantee of tomorrow and enjoy the moment.' It wasn't far after this that I was using pain killers such as Percocet, Xanax, Vicodin, and OxyContin, regularly to drown out the pain of losing my brother. I developed a hatred for myself, and a lack of confidence set in, which fueled the addiction even further. I had gotten to the point of needing to sell drugs and working odd jobs until about the age of 21. This was when I had tried heroin for the first time, and I began to enter the point of no return. When people asked me how I was doing, I would respond with, "Living the dream one drink at a time." I was far from that. Between getting so drunk, I would black out, forget stuff I did, and pee on the bed. I was so drunk and in total self-destruction mode. I did what I could afford to get high or drunk and became a regular user of heroin by the age of 22. It was at that point that people started to notice my unusual behaviors more and more.

Thankfully, my mom was the investigator who found my stash of dope and was setting up an intervention. However, at the last minute, my dad decided against surprising me with that and told me about it before dropping me off at my mom's house. I immediately left and went to get some dope, but secretly, I was relieved that I could finally get the help I have wanted for so long. I was embarrassed and ashamed but knew deep down I needed the help. I remember sitting there and crying with my mom, saying, "I am ready, I can't live this way any longer." The next day, I was on a plane to Phoenix, AZ. I, of course, did some drugs before taking off on this new journey at the age of 25, and my official sobriety date is October 2nd, 2015. I entered into a six-month program with New Freedom in Prescott, AZ. This is where I learned to process my feelings in a healthy manner and face some of the demons plaguing me for some time. However, I ended up getting asked to leave after five months due to some disagreements between the staff and I about my amends trip that was a part of the program. This started when my mom was willing to provide me with her car that she was getting rid of, and we planned to do a fun road trip from Wisconsin to Arizona. They argued that I wasn't ready to make amends and that I was using my brother's passing as a leverage to receive help from my mom. Despite what they said, I did not get angry and just knew in my heart that it was time for me to depart. My mom was nervous and scared as any mother would be as I embarked on living out of my car, hopping couch to couch for the next couple of months. At this point, I was working multiple jobs and was fortunate my sponsor at the time allowed me to stay on his couch for a month because I got to a point I was ready to move back home because I wouldn't continue couch surfing. Then, I found a place, it wasn't the greatest, but it was a place to rest my head at night.

Not soon after, I received an opportunity to get out of Prescott and move to Phoenix for a job at the same company my dad works for, but he is in Wisconsin. This meant packing up what little I had and trying to start over again in a new city. I was fortunate enough that my cousin happened to be moving down after getting out of college to become a teacher and allowed me to stay in her one-bedroom apartment. Eventually, I had gotten my own place off craigslist. It was a fully furnished room. I couldn't afford a better apartment because, at this point, I had ruined my credit score and that deterred me from getting a better apartment.

Not soon after getting my own place, I was back to

working multiple jobs; 7-days a week, including a house manager position at a recovery center. I always had a niche for helping others and always told the guys I didn't need to be here; I wanted to be here. Things were looking up and my life continued to get even better because I kept a positive attitude and didn't give up. This next part is when I had gone on the first date with my now wife, Kimberly. People thought we were crazy on how fast we moved in our relationship, and after three months of dating, we moved in together. We both knew that we were the one for each other and felt like we had known each other for years. Most importantly, she had accepted me for being the ex-addict/alcoholic I was and saw the greatness inside of me. I truly believe that we were destined to meet, and even though we are polar opposites, we got married on October 12th, 2019. It was just after my 4 years in sobriety, and we have been through a lot together and have a strong bond because of those situations.

I have briefly explained in this book some major events that have helped shape the man you read about in this book of overcoming anything against all odds. This story aims to help the others who abuse(d) drugs and alcohol and struggle to pick up the pieces after. I am an advocate for seeing the light come on for people and give them hope that an ex-addict was able to change the course of his life by first changing his mindset, having a positive attitude, always staying focused on where I wanted to go but remaining flexible in my approaches. I always stay humble, sharing love with everyone I encounter, continuously exceeding myself every day, and trusting the universe will provide me with what I do and do not need in my life. It has been an honor and a privilege to be a part of this amazing book series and share my story with those reading this book. I hope that my story can take away the stigma behind drug and alcohol addiction. I believe it will help us see that we work just as hard if not harder than the people that judged us, that deep down, we are all human beings that deserve the same love and respect as you would give to your loved ones. I have proven to those that have read my words that beyond a shadow of a doubt, anyone can move mountains and make magic happen by just believing in themselves and not giving up when life throws its jabs at you. We can overcome anything if we're willing to make the effort and be receptive to new information. I have had some hardships along the way but will continue to help the next person to the best of my ability.

About the Author

Upon this book being published, Sean Timothy Steiner will have graduated with a Bachelor's Degree in Business Administration with concentration in Information Systems Management from Purdue University Global. He started his own business working with a previous author from the first volume of this book series, Kohdi Rayne for the Beyond Sober aspect.

Sean is a sobriety coach, servant leader, and brand ambassador with Beyond Sober, the largest sobriety movement since AA. He has started a nonprofit organization with a business partner to help recovering addicts build valuable life skills. He has also started his own clothing brand, developed his own master platform to turn others into super humans. He is also working on a treatment center/animal rescue, and other ventures. He is amazingly blessed to have risen from the darkness to unlock his light. He is delighted that he can share his story with you today. You can find all about Sean by connecting via his website, and if you know anyone who might be struggling, please reach out to Sean and he will do everything he can to help.

Website: www.thewiscokid.com
Email: wiscokid@beyondsobercoach.com
wiscokid89@gmial.com

Carmen Ventrucci

CHAPTER SEVEN

ALL YOU HAVE TO DO IS ASK

Have you ever noticed that some people just seem to get everything they want? Little things, big things... things always seem to work out for them. Or, are you one of these people? I've been noticing this a lot more lately, and I'm starting to pay attention as to why.

My husband and I like to watch TV together in the evenings. It's our time to unwind after the kids have gone to bed, laugh, and discuss the shows we're watching.

One commonality I've noticed in the shows we've seen over the past two weeks is that things always seem to just work out. And not because it's the writing and they're going for a joke or wrapping up the storyline with a nice bow, it's because things are actually working out.

We watched the pilot episode of Friends last night. Early in the episode, Ross, played by Davis Schimmer, says, "I don't want to be single, okay? I just... I just- I just wanna be married again!" And in walks Rachel, played by Jennifer Aniston, in a wedding dress, soaking wet from the rain.

Hmmm, that just seemed to work out. Ross asked for something, and it showed up, seemingly out of the blue.

We rewatched the Entourage series. Vinny Chase and Eric Murphy were discussing a heated situation in Season 8, Episode 4. Eric says, "Things always work out for us, Vince. We will get through this, and it will work out. I guarantee it!"

It turns out things did work out by the end of the episode. Hmmmmm, that just seems to work out there too, and with the bonus of unshakable certainty.

Then yesterday, I spoke with my client, Lea. She had new stories of how something she wanted had come true. This is nothing new; Lea is filled with stories like this. She seems to be the queen of getting what she asks for. However, this time, I was paying more attention due to my recent TV watching. I listened to her, and my jaw dropped in awe. How does she keep doing this?

She wanted her daughter to move across the country and be closer to her. It happened.

She wanted some money and found some in her jacket pocket.

She wanted her son to give her back the emotional baggage she gave him, he did.

And that is just the tip of the iceberg.

OK, now I was paying attention, and I was curious. I just had three examples of people creating the future they want, and I had to know how this was happening. Granted, two examples were fictional, and the topic has still grabbed my attention.

How do some people seem to make anything they want to occur? How do some people just seem to have everything work out? And, how do I do that too?

I started asking Lea questions, probing her for more information and insight. I was curious.

"Lea," I said, "what's going on? How are you making all of these things come to fruition?"

"I manifested them," she replied.

"What does that mean?" I asked.

"It's really simple. Manifestation is asking for what you want and being open to how it shows up," Lea said.

The emotional part of my brain was intrigued. The logical, skeptical part of my brain started to kick in too. "Wait, isn't this that 'woo woo' stuff? Think positive thoughts and positive things happen? Think negative thoughts and negative things happen?" I asked.

"Actually, you're onto something," Lea replied. "I do see that all the time in other people and myself. Those with a negative outlook tend to encounter more negative experiences. They complain a lot. Those who think positively tend to have more positive experiences. Our brains are wired for negativity, it's a survival mechanism, so I understand that it's not easy to be positive all the time. I find that any positivity helps.'

"So you walk around with positive thoughts all the time?" I asked.

"No, I'm not perfect, and I do believe in myself, and that anything is possible," said Lea. "It's like that famous Henry Ford Quote. *" Whether you think you can or you can't-you're right."* It emphasizes the belief that you can do something or the belief that something can occur. I apply this same logic to manifesting. If I believe I can, then I can. If I believe I can't, then I will not be able to manifest."

"OK," I said slowly as I was processing everything Lea just said. "What's your process? Tell me how you actually do this? How do you manifest?"

"Sometimes I think of what I want, and I say it out loud. 'It would be really cool if this happened.' Then I let it go."

Ignoring the chorus of Elsa singing "Let it Go" from Frozen that immediately popped into my head, I asked more questions. "What do you mean you let it go?"

"I speak it. I like to actually speak it instead of just thinking it in my head, and then I let it go. I ask for what I want, and I'm then open to how it shows up for me. But, I have to remember to be careful for what I wish for. Once, a while back, I wished my 18-year-old son would get a job and move out of my house. My vision was him living nearby, and I wasn't specific enough in my request. He ended up joining the Marine Corp, moving far away for four years, and I was worried about him every day. Did he move out of the house and get a job? Yes. Was it the way I wanted? No. Plus, it was my choice to worry. That's one of the keys to manifesting. You have to be open to and receive the outcome. And, you have to be specific about what you want."

"Huh," I said, considering what Lea just said. "I can see why being specific is important; otherwise, things might show up for you in a creative way. How do you get more specific? Do you make a list?"

"I don't make a list, and I am working on being more specific," replied Lea. "I already told you about how I wasn't specific about my son moving out of my home and getting a job, and he ended up joining the Marine Corp. Another time I wasn't specific right before I moved to New York. I decided I was going to win the lottery. The thing is, I said 'lottery' and not 'jackpot.' I won $1. Technically, I won the lottery, just not the extreme that I wanted." Lea and I giggled at this; you have to admit that's funny. "Now I write down things I want sometimes and look to see if I'm missing anything. I might have someone else look at it too for a second set of eyes."

This conversation was amazing, and I had to play devil's advocate for a moment. "So you're telling me that I can say something like, 'I'm going to make a ton of money in my business, joyfully, by the end of this year,' and that will happen?"

"Yes," Lea replied. "But first, my intuition says that the statement is not specific enough. How much is 'a ton of money?' That could be different for everyone. And second, you have to believe in the outcome completely. And that is the key. You have to be **certain**. You have to believe that the outcome is possible with your entire being. 'A ton of money' might not be believable for you because it could be a big jump from where you are today. Everyone manifests differently, you have to understand how manifestation works for you. And, you have to let go of the need to please people. I manifest some things that other people would consider ridiculous. I don't care what others think or say about what I believe because they are my beliefs. I create my reality."

"Interesting," I responded. "Is part of your success in manifesting acting as if the outcome is going to happen?

Take the lottery, for example, did you start acting like you won the lottery before you won the lottery?"

"Not necessarily," said Lea. "It's not a matter of acting as if for me because now I'm paying attention to the fact that I am manifesting what I'm asking for. I have realized that I know it is coming, I am certain it is coming, and I am open to how it arrives. It's more about being certain than anything else. I am certain things will show up for me. I am certain. I create my reality. I am certain everything will happen the way that it is meant to."

"Another interesting thing," Lea continued, "occasionally when manifesting things for myself, I realized it wasn't the best. So, I manifested a change. Recently, I thought it would be really cool to live in this one specific apartment, so I manifested it, and it happened. After living there for about three months, I realized the apartment wasn't the best option for me. Once I realized that, I manifested moving out. Guess what, another opportunity presented itself, and I was able to move out. You can change your mind, as I did, and you can use manifestation to help get you to where you need to be."

Wow, I thought to myself. That is extremely powerful. And, there was something familiar about that statement. My memory started racing. I began recalling things and the feelings and emotions associated with events I had manifested in my past.

In 2016, I won a global award for a project I lead because I manifested it. I distinctly remember being at the awards ceremony for the previous winner, and I decided that I would win next year. I didn't know how, or for what project, and I decided I would win anyway. I believed. I was certain of the outcome, I acted as if success was inevitable, and I figured it out along the way. I manifested that award, along with the right project, the right challenge to solve, and the right team to help me solve it. There was a feeling of absolute and associated confidence that this would happen. There was no doubt in my mind.

I manifested my nieces coming to live with me. When they were much younger, I vividly recall saying that they could always come to live with us, no questions asked. Now, about ten years later, we have welcomed them into our home and are proud to be their legal guardians. It was as if I knew; I was certain that would occur one day.

"Lea, one last question," I stated. "What happens if something you manifest never happens? Then what?"

"If I'm working on manifesting something and it doesn't happen, it's one of two things," Lea replied. "One, I'm not ready for it. Or two, it has no place in my life. When this happens, I take a look at what I'm manifesting again and reconsider it. Is this something I really want, or is it not in my highest and greatest interest? Usually, once I don't manifest something I'm asking for, I realize it won't serve me, and I let it go."

Lea and I chatted for a bit longer, talked about her progress as my client, then hung up the phone. I reflected on what we talked about.

It's OK to ask for what you want, so go ahead and ask.

Believe in what you want.

Be specific about what you want.

Be certain it will come to you.

Be flexible in how it shows up.

About two hours later, I got a phone call from another mom. My 9-year-old daughter was watching her friends play in a softball tournament and her friend's mom gave me the update. In the second game of the tournament, the opposing team was missing a few players. They asked anyone watching if they wanted to play. My daughter, being the outgoing child she is, volunteered and immediately joined the game.

"You should have seen her," said the other mom. "She has so much fun playing softball. And do you know what the funny part is? During the first game, she said, 'I hope another team is short players so I can play softball today.' She said it, and it came true!"

I smiled while I was on the phone, that proud mother smile one gets when their child does something spectacular. After my amazing conversation with Lea, this phone call tied it all together. My daughter just manifested the opportunity to play softball. She threw the thought out there and played with certainty.

Pay attention to how you make things a reality for you. I'm glad I did. I know I've manifested in the past, and now I have a new perspective on how to do more of it better. **Walk with certainty**, know that you create your reality, and believe in your outcomes.

Now, go manifest something great.

About the Author

Carmen Ventrucci helps entrepreneurs and business owners shed restrictions and do what they truly want in life. She has built her life and business around this concept and shows her clients how to do the same. She loves elevating businesses to the next level and is called "The Girl with the Golden Shovel" due to the results she helps her clients produce. Carmen embodies SISU, a Finnish term meaning grit, determination, and tenacity, no matter the obstacles, no matter the odds. Carmen, her husband, and her family of six kids are currently touring the USA in an RV while road-schooling, building businesses, and having fun. They created a business, The Ruby Road, to document their story and you can follow their adventures on YouTube.

To learn more about Carmen visit www.TrueSisuLife.com and www.TheRubyRoad.com

Julie Williams

CHAPTER EIGHT

THIS IS ME

We all have many stories in our lives. Some good, some bad, some ugly. Stories we tell. Stories people gossip about. And stories never to be spoken of. Stories of repeated patterns, events that change our lives, and situations that afford us the opportunity to grow.

So if I may, I'd like to share with you; just one story from my life

The location where my tale begins is an Art Deco and Gothic-inspired office and retail building. One of the most prominent and best-known buildings in Melbourne, the iconic Manchester Unity Building.

I stood waiting for the elevator with only thoughts of the supplies I needed; I was oblivious to my surroundings. The copper-clad doors slide open, and I was presented with a familiar face. It was a happy reunion. We had met years earlier when I had done some work for him.

Back then, I'd moved out of town for what I thought was a wonderful relationship only to be left betrayed, broken-hearted, and completely lost.

Now that I had returned to my hometown, he and I agreed to keep in contact. A few months or so later, I began working for him. Firstly, from home and then in the shop dealing with his customers. He listened as I told my tales of sorrow.

I never thought I would be a business owner, yet within six months he'd convinced me, and the business was mine. My only option. My new adventure. Happy days ahead.

More than sixteen years my senior, he stood straight and probably a foot taller than me. He was a man I believed to be my friend, a guiding light, and somehow my protector.

I kept the business name the same, feeling safe in someone else's shadow. My self-worth had taken a battering from the breakup. The thought of putting myself out there did not even register.

He seemed to have a great life. I planned on having the same. How lucky was I?

Fast forward a few years. I was always working and still doing the same as he. The same open hours. The same clients. The same Melbourne runs to suppliers. I had made work my priority. I had little time for anything else.

Customers were used to me by now, and we always enjoyed a good chat. If we weren't talking about work, we were speaking about travel. This was my escape. I planned a holiday each year, and a travel companion would present themselves. I wasn't ready to date, so each time, a different friend would come along. We would have such a great time; so much fun. This was the life.

Before one such trip, I had asked him to help out with work while I was away. It was agreed, and I was grateful. A few weeks after I returned, a customer contacted me. She had collected her goods from him, and she believed something was missing. My thoughts, too, so I asked him about it. Apparently, I hadn't charged enough for the job, so he'd taken it upon himself to redeem his costs.

The tone in his voice was different. It was the first time I'd noticed. Why couldn't we have a normal conversation about it? Why couldn't he simply charge me for it? I couldn't believe he had the audacity, the brazenness to steal from my customer. The item was gone.

This was my business. Yes, this was my business. Old patterns of beating myself up raised their ugly head, and my self-talk was all negative. I am to blame. I should never have gone away. I failed my customer.

Nothing I said or offered in replacement was enough to take her sadness away. The cost was irrelevant. The sentiment was everything. Customer lost, lesson learned, trust no one.

I'm not sure if I was wearing rose-coloured glasses or if he had been wearing a mask, but I did know that my view of him was changing.

While attending a seminar a friend asked me to, I discovered personality archetypes. How interesting. Curious and keen for more knowledge, I booked into a one-day event. I spent the day soaking up the information, nodding my head, and agreeing with everything. Before leaving that day, I signed up for a truly amazing roller coaster ride of personal growth: transformational coaching, NLP (Neuro Linguistic Programming), fabulous new friends and travel. It was eye opening, mind-expanding, and seemed brand new to me. I loved it and it was a taste of possibilities.

He came into work one day presenting me with paperwork. He was asking for more money in addition to the rent. He used some excuse for the increase. It made no sense to me. I decided to look into it. What was the reason behind it? Was it greed? Was it power play?

I didn't understand what I had done wrong. Why was he treating me differently? Why was he dismissing all my findings? He was becoming angry. Why did I deserve this? Was this the behaviour of a narcissist losing control of someone else's mind?

Once upon a time, I would have just said yes and tried to make everything better. However, this time, I chose to listen to my intuition, and I said no. I'm sure he found my resistance unexpected, and it surprised me too—a line crossed for both of us. There was no going back.

Looking into the lease led me to see very clearly just what had been happening. My lawyers informed me I had been conned in every possible way. The sale of the alleged business. The rental contract itself. Even the terms and conditions. The broker he introduced me to was also in on the act and had organized a very dodgy business loan. The bank approved a loan that today (especially after the Royal Banking Commission) would never be valid. All of them were taking their piece of me.

He continued exposing unattractive qualities. His darkness flowed more, and stand-over tactics began. As if I didn't hate myself enough, he was a constant reminder. His words were mean and cruel. His tone was powerful. You signed your f***ing life away. Without this place, you are nothing. There were even threats against my personal safety. I mean really... I am five foot 1 ½.

Have you ever noticed that blowing out someone else's candle doesn't make yours shine any brighter?

Even when I changed the locks under legal advice, he

continued his appalling behaviour. He was threatening to break down the door at work, barging into my lawyer's office and abusing his staff. He was acting like a five-year-old who didn't get his way.

He seemed to be in his element, loving every second and strutting around in his relentless pursuit of superiority. He and his false sense of entitlement became so unbearable my only option was to vacate the premises. Keeping my customers' goods safe was my priority, then getting myself out of harm's way.

Negotiations began through legal teams regarding the end of the lease. We were fighting over the phone number, my ability to attend for open days, and leaving my new details on the front window. The drama continued as I looked for another shop premises.

The following week, he did the unthinkable and opened the shop. He proceeded to tell stories from his erratic mind to anyone who would listen. Stories that he was the owner and he always had been. He told them that I had sold all the customers' goods and had taken off overseas. He said that I left town owing him money and that his legal team couldn't find me. My favourite was when he told my cousin I was driving around in a brand-new BMW.

There were lots of phone calls from customers: some understanding, and some not.

Most people saw through him; he only lasted three weeks.

I felt alone, confused, and extremely embarrassed. I'd been groomed, ripped off, and humiliated. I never wanted anyone to know or see me like this, but I'm sure the cracks were showing. I was ashamed of my vulnerability. How did I allow someone to treat me so poorly? When did I give all of my power away?

There was a lot of running around delivering goods and making house calls before I found a place to rent. In the new shop, there was money to be spent and work to be done. Creation began with a new business name, a different shop setup, and a colourful logo. This was an exciting time for me; a burst of happiness. Although most of the time, I struggled to complete any work at all. I was feeling deflated, mentally exhausted, and crushed inside. My self-worth and energy were at an all-time low. My bank account balance was even lower. Yet, in some way, I was proud I made it out.

For a while, I considered he had won, and I wanted to give up. Imagine being defeated in a game I didn't even know I was playing.

My bucket was being filled faster than I could empty it. On top of work issues, my dad was diagnosed with a life-threatening illness. It was unbelievable, and I wondered what would come next.

I found myself in the dark night of the soul; a place only I could bring myself out of. The pain of staying the same had outweighed the pain of change, so I chose to let go of the person I was.

The coaching was my go-to when I had the chance, and I did my best to keep up. Most times, my conscious mind couldn't deal with the pressure. Thinking back, I had completely underestimated the power of the subconscious or unconscious mind. I now know mine had been holding the fort.

I had become aware of who I didn't want to be. The next step was to become the person I did want to be. There were challenges, of course.

One particular day, I walked into a trade shop only to see him right before me at the counter. So much for his retirement. Yuk, my skin crawled, and I felt nauseous. I couldn't get out of there quick enough. Calming down over lunch, I continued on to the next shop. Talking over the counter with a salesperson, I noticed a dark figure coming straight towards me out of the corner of my eye. He was between me and the exit. I could feel his creepy energy, but I didn't flinch. I needed him to see me unaffected by his presence, so I continued my conversation, adding a laugh or two. When I didn't take the bait, he moved away into the shadows and I was free to leave.

I knew my spiritual awareness was increasing. In fact, my mind had been expanding all along. I was finally beginning to understand and experience energy and connection.

After years of little involvement, I began practicing Reiki again. My toolbox already had some great tools; I simply needed to use them.

I came to a wonderful realization. Staying in your comfort zone is good; however, straying from your comfort zone is better. By going out of your comfort zone, you actually expand it thus giving yourself the opportunity to experience more potential. Enjoy and embrace the challenge.

Imagine this; you're walking along a path and you see a snake ahead of you. Instead of running away in fear, you have a closer look and realize it's only a stick. The threat is now gone, and you are free to move forward along your path. The great thing is, once you know it's a stick, you can never see it as a snake again.

It was the week before Christmas. The elevator opened, it's empty, and I jumped in. I was going up, but I had a sinking feeling. I was meant to be going down. The Universe always has a plan.

The copper-clad doors slide open, and once again, I was presented with a familiar face. He stopped in his tracks, released a huge sigh, and entered the elevator. It's just the two of us. I actually felt OK. I was so proud of myself.

The silence was deafening, so I started speaking. My words were polite and straightforward. My face was plain and emotionless. He had greyer hair, shrunken shoulders and was shorter than I remembered.

The mighty winner of the game. Through my eyes, broken and powerless. A fitting end to this cycle, complete at the elevator of the Manchester Unity Building.

And as I walked out to the street looking up, I saw the clouds had gone. The sky was blue, and I felt the sunshine on my face. Fulfilling the final stage of this hero's journey, here I was venturing back out into the world as the person I want to be.

Knowing that '*When You Walk With Certainty,*' possibilities are all around.

The stories we each have make us who we are today. And they influence who we will become. We can choose to use our experiences in many ways.

I could have curled up in a ball and never come out of the dark.

I could be driving the karma train, going full steam ahead and shouting TOOT! TOOT!

However, I chose to exit the drama cycle, expand my mind and learn.

With over seven billion people on this planet, what circumstances brought this person into my life? What was being mirrored to me? What was my lesson? I considered our similarities. Was I like him, what did we have in common, and how had I treated people before? Thinking this way, I could understand to some extent, the reasons for his behaviour. Hurt people, hurt people.

I also considered my position as an easy target and knew I never wanted to be taken advantage of again. I learned to be at cause for myself. I found my inner strength.

Taking all emotion out, I believe we both wanted to feel good about ourselves. Being a business owner made me feel good. Treating people badly somehow made him feel good. Feeling good was the connection, the thing we had in common. We had the same destination, just different ways of getting there.

The feeling of emotions is an amazing learning guide. To me, positive emotions say I'm on the right track and I embrace them. They vibrate higher energetically and lift you up. Negative emotions show me I have work to do. Is this emotion passing through, or do I feel it all the time? What do I want instead, what do I need to do, and how do I need to behave? Do I have the tools to do this, or can I learn something new? Negative emotions vibrate lower and can act like an anchor weighing you down or a distraction holding you back. So if they don't serve you, cut them loose. Reach out, raise your vibration, and rise above.

I have learned a better use of words and language. 'Should' is a word I do my best not to use anymore. Also, the intention behind words can be very powerful. We can use it to control, influence or make someone's day. Just tell someone they have a great smile and see how much joy you can bring.

I choose to create in myself, the qualities I admire in others. I love strength, so I want to be strong myself. I love kindness, so I want to be kind to others and kind to myself. I now enjoy the most wonderful people in my life and move on from those who weigh me down.

I choose to grow my awareness and see from different perspectives. Even when my earnings were at their lowest, I still booked myself on a holiday. I wasn't abundant in cash; I was abundant in adventure.

Has my story put me off men? No way. I believe men are magnificent.

At the very least, they certainly have the potential, as

every person has. But sometimes there's a little bit of arsehole thrown in, and sometimes there's a lot.

I choose to make a positive out of a negative. Within the timeline of my story, I have learned that I am a visual, kinesthetic learner and a three times convincer. And usually a mis-matcher. I am clairsentient, somewhat clairvoyant, and my talent archetype is Magician. The magician/alchemist – a person who transforms or creates through a seemingly magical process. Wow!

Discovering this information is simply priceless. I encourage everyone to learn all they can about themselves. It is absolutely incredible what can be discovered.

I found both my worst enemy and my greatest support within ME. Perhaps we are only given problems we already know how to solve. Sometimes you see the solution easily, and sometimes you have to go searching. Either way, you are worth it.

Why look for someone to feed you a fish when you can become your own fisherman. Feel free to be your own knight in shining armour.

You can choose to put your oxygen mask on first, and then lead the way in service to others. You never know who might need your light to bring them out of their darkness. You never know who might need your light to see.

Did I save the whole world? No, but I saved mine. When I think of whom I was a decade, five years, or even six months ago, it seems like lifetimes have passed. If we choose to, we can be forever evolving, connecting, and expanding. We can align our thoughts, emotions, and actions in creating our lives. We can choose to thrive.

If I want the freedom to pursue my passions and love my life, then I choose to accept that freedom in others. We all have different strengths, ideas and actions, we have different definitions of right and wrong, good and bad.

That's the beauty of it. How boring would life be if we were all the same?

Be kind to yourself, be true to yourself, and you will shine.

Today, I am in my new studio, a creation of my own. It's fresh and bright, comfortable and friendly. It is a place where I've reminded myself I can dream. A place of new opportunities; I love it.

I hope somewhere through reading this, you may have made a connection, experienced an emotion, or simply filled in part of your day. Either way, I thank you for your time. It's the most precious gift we have.

This is just one story from my life.

This is real.

This is me.

About the Author

Julie Williams resides in Geelong, Victoria, Australia.

Julie (Jules) has been a Jeweler for over 25 years, and her business "Jewels In Life" specializes in custom jewelry hand makes representing life events.

Jules is a certified Transformational Life Coach, practicing Reiki energy healer and first-time author.

She is a salsa dancing crystal enthusiast who loves to travel, taking inspiration from destinations across the globe.

For further information please visit

www.jewelsinlife.com

Guinevere Smith

CHAPTER NINE

WALK IN MY UNIVERSE

I know you have heard that the only things that are certain in life are death and taxes. While those are true, you can then *walk with certainty* when you dig deep and hard on your purpose. Imagine making the time to truly get into one's self to not only think about what you want, deciding what that is, and then going for it. This sounds terrifying to the old me. It is scary. How many of you have done it already? I don't blame you if you haven't yet. My hope for this chapter is that it gets you to really think about your life and walk with certainty. If not, then my wish for you is to gain tools to think about and find the courage to GO FOR IT!

There are certainly different degrees of these types of decisions. Colleges, careers, relationships commitments, and family desires to name a few. However, how many of you made decisions based on what you "thought" was expected of you or what you perceived to be the right answer? OH! This hit me hard. I am so guilty of this. I am a recovering people pleaser. A child-like human who knew the rules and followed them in fear of disappointment or shame. I feel this question in the pit of my stomach. I know I'm not the only one. We have a social life, family, and self-expectations that surround us every day. There are constant judgments from others. It is the self-judgment I have only recently begun to unravel like the layers of an onion. Some make me want to cry like I'm chopping a fragrant one for my favorite Thai dish.

First, a little background on me to set the scene and help you understand how far I have actually come to date. Enter whatever your background looks like, in reality, no one is that different: different chapter; different story but the same idea.

A long distant time ago, all I wanted to do was meet someone, marry, and begin a family. That's what you do, right? I moved south and met my "southern gentleman," or so I thought. We wedded at the young age of 24. Check! I truly thought this is what I was supposed to do. We decided to start a family a year into our marriage. Check! We had some fertility issues. Ummmm, not check! That's not what is expected of me. Insert massive judgment, disappointment, and shame. After a few short months of fertility drugs, we were pregnant. Check! Back on track, so to speak. My husband and I started a small lawn care business.

Entrepreneurship.... Check! We were bumping along life as a family. Life was great, right? Add three miscarriages and two more babies. Boom! Check! Suddenly after the birth of my third child, I was overly aware I was not happy. Fast forward eight years, and I skip and sing through my every day with certainty. I know that is almost comical. As I reread that paragraph, I laughed and thought if only it was that easy. I want to take you along for that ride discovering the tools that got me there. It wasn't easy or even pretty. I am also not going to lie to you and tell you it's all roses from here. It is constant work on myself. A complete and total commitment to accept nothing less than what I desire or deserve. Even then, I adjust and redirect my energy to new ideas and aspirations. This experience will flood you with doubt and limiting beliefs. It's owning your shit and working through it. Then honestly, it's being brave enough to trust and believe in yourself. That simple; however, complicated too.

When I truly stepped into my power was on the side of a mountain in Glacier National Park in Montana. I decided to invest in myself energetically this time. Last year, I was on a healing journey. This year was all about balancing, centering, and raising my vibrations. Nothing to do with business per se. However, it was a need that was felt in my core. Makes sense, right? I needed to center my core existence before I felt I could decide about my career or even myself. I made the decision with absolute certainty that I needed this mastermind in the middle of nowhere, in a state I knew nobody or anything with a small group of humans I had never met. Okay, I attended with a soul sister

I had met twice but knew through Facebook group and lots of phone calls and texts. You get the point, though. This kind of experience I set myself up for was not my norm. In the past, just the idea of what I was about to embark on would have given me anxiety for weeks leading up to it. Not this occasion; I was quietly pumped and ready for the transformation that was beginning to stir in my universe.

Seven energized beings gathered at the airport all within an hour of each other and hailed each other like old friends and not strangers. Little did we know, we had just found our tribe. This diversified group immediately fed my soul.

They taught me how to sit quietly in my thoughts. What?! No way was I prepared to do that. Up until then, I lived in chaos. Up until then, I thrived under pressure. Up until then, I procrastinated so much I didn't have time to sit in silence. I believe up until then, I was addicted to the stress of chaos. I was proud of the robust and fierce energy. I did my best work under pressure persona. It did not, though, serve my constant call for peace, calm, and balance. Acknowledging and unlocking this belief was life changing.

So then, what was next? Our leader believed we had to dump all of our fears and limitations. He chose meditation and a journal to help us dump these restraints. We drove out to a hiking path, fill ammunition containers up with rocks and our pieces of paper with our scribbled fears. We were then instructed to carry that box up the mountain and ask for help when we need it. I had some choice thoughts about this little exercise because asking for help was a serious default and weakness of mine. (Not in the way you think, just in the yeah, I have a hard time doing this;

however has turned into a skill to strengthen and watch it grow in power.) On top of that, my hiking experiences in the past had been to prove to myself what I was made of physically. This was to show mentality and vulnerability. When I made that connection (and was out of breath), I turned around and asked for help. This action alone was physically painful. In fact, it came out in massive emotions. I cried for the next five minutes.

Ironically, I felt lighter suddenly. These humans were there to assist. They would not judge, they understood the struggle, and they loved me unconditionally already. I would have extended myself for any one of them in a split nanosecond. Why hesitate? I believe conditioning is why. My past trauma had taught me not to ask for help. It was not safe to do so. In the past, 95% of the time, it was used against me either immediately or stored as ammunition. That was my current story. As easy as it was to explain why it was my current story, it became that easy to change. The emotional response was a cleansing of sorts, and it felt like I lifted 20 pounds off my shoulders. It wasn't just the rocks, either. Friends even said that afternoon how young my face was suddenly. It was that immediate. I was that certain that I just changed my entire existence. It was only the beginning, though. When we reached our destination, we read our fears and then burned the hell out of them. It was so accurate how each piece of paper took on the flame of the lighter. Each confessional paper danced differently. Some resisted the flame, while others caught immediately and flared high.

The next adventure of the day was to plunge into the cold, 38–43-degree lake. To say this experience was riveting isn't quite right. So much excitement, fear, nerves, and joy wrap in one jumpy body. I did it. I dove in head-first. Nothing life-changing happened here except my call to cold immersion baths and dips for health benefits. Beyond that, I just knew that fear was not stopping me from taking part in this audacious event. Talk about certainty. That is something I decided for myself a year ago.... Fear is not real. I decided I wanted to take a chance on something I perceived as scary every day. In fact, I have a magnet with that quote from Eleanor Roosevelt on it. My son, just the other day, while staring at something he was hesitant about, asked me, "Momma, should I really do something that scares me every day?" I responded lovingly and supportively, "Yes baby, I like to live my life that way! However, you need to decide for yourself." There is no wrong answer here. I'm proud to say my son was very brave at that moment and shares his story often.

The next morning, I woke up very uneasy and overwhelmed. My unconscious mind must have been hard at work over night, processing everything I had taken in the previous day. I was jumpy, distracted, and emotional. I was in no way prepared for the damnation that was coming my way. I knew it too. I shared with the group how I was feeling. This was supposed to be a good idea since they had been encouraging all of those feelings, talks, and asking for help. Well, a new one had entered our dynamic, and he was full of all-knowing, let's get to the bottom of this hard-headed nut. While I didn't much appreciate his style, I was able to tap into my newfound energy, separate my feelings about him, and take all of the good that was being thrown at me.

I was told that I was beyond wise and I had mastered the dance of distraction. It was shared with me that until I realized that it's only me holding me back, I will stay stuck. I was like this newborn superhero being backed into a corner. I instantaneously puffed out my chest and armored up and looked at myself in all of my glory and knew with no doubt that I was truly unstoppable. I no longer felt doubt or fear that I was going to manifest every last damn thing I declared I wanted. That's a certainty! How to figure out what I wanted was a different story.

When someone inquires and asks you what you want, how easy is it to answer? Be honest! Do you know with every ounce of your being with no hesitation? Do you have an idea, but you can take or leave it? No biggie. Maybe it actually hurts your head to think about what you want? It seems too foreign to express your deepest darkest desires. Do your friends and family support your yearnings, or do they judge them? One of my favorite thoughts is, you say I dream too big, I say you think too small. Sometimes it is just a simple mindset shift. I like to be different, so if people think I am crazy, it solidifies I'm on the right path.

How does one uncover their vision that is so unique and precise? You have to allow quiet in your day. Most fancy people call it meditating. I know; I have jokes. Mediation, up until now, was an outlandish concept. Meditation is the habitual process of training your mind to focus and redirect your thoughts. Tell that to my ADHD brain. In the past, I would sit there in a chilled pose and chant, think of nothing. Only think of space. Then, SQUIRREL moment would happen and BAM! I am in a new direction. I mean, this is literally how it would go and just as quickly as you read those few sentences. When I say, I understand the challenge of sitting in my thoughts and focusing, I truly mean it.

In the past years of healing, I used guided meditations to fall asleep at night. That is one sure-fire way NOT to learn to zone in on your thoughts. I could even practice a guided meditation sitting up and manage to fall asleep. I know; I am talented.

What clicked for me was learning to harvest my energy and sit in it. That was more delicate of a skill for me. Particularly with my eyes closed. Visualization and grounding help me to develop that dexterity. Visualization is the formation of mental images or the process of interpreting in visual terms. Visualization is one of the best ways to get your mind back on track when you feel out of balance. I used to think of this only in terms of daydreaming. However, sitting in the morning, visualizing my day and how it's going to play out is a form of meditation. Who knew right?

Grounding, also known as earthing, has many benefits. First, we must understand it is the simplicity of being connected to the earth. Grounding yourself is the process of balancing your physical, emotional, mental, and energy state and reconnecting them. We do this in many ways. The most obvious and popular method is getting your bare feet planted in the grass or dirt. Gardening has the same effects. Other suggestions are placing your hand in water, breathing deeply, taking a walk, holding ice, feeling your body, listening to your surroundings, playing music, or even touching something comforting. It is not hard to notice; this act involves your senses. So you can see how it might balance you. I came to realize I was doing a lot of these things already to soothe myself throughout the day. Look at me, I can actually meditate.

The next challenge was to declare time for myself to

do this beautiful sign of self-love. I also knew from experience that I couldn't assume I would suddenly be able to stay sharp for 60 minutes right out the gate. I was kind to myself and began with one-minute increments, 3-5 times a day. I was also not foolish to believe I would remember to do this five times a day. I set reminders and alarms on my phone. I began to look forward to those moments that I got to stop what I was doing and center myself. I heard this remarkable tip while in Montana about fire meditation. No more information was needed for me. I love staring at a campfire in a trance. I carry a lighter with me now, and it's not because I have three packs a day habit. Nope! It is an escape I have designed and stick to in my new freedom schedule. Other than that, I have votive candles ready to go in the house. Now I can manage a 10–15-minute mediation but still enjoy my 1-minute fire stares.

Why do I share these strategies of quiet? It is from here that magic begins. I kept thinking all of these amazing thoughts and breakthroughs would happen in only the muted sessions. However, my biggest a-ha moments occurred during other activities. I would be doing a set of dishes and a thought would come through like a lightning bolt, and I am left there dumbstruck saying out loud, "Would you look at that? interesting...." My favorite most recent clarity thoughts were about my limiting beliefs around money. Up until now, I had a fixed mindset about money. I have begun saying affirmations like, "I am abundant in money" or "Money flows to me easily." While doing this the other day, I heard myself say, "I will take responsibility of my money." I was cleaning the countertops in my kitchen, and it stopped me dead in my tracks. Who in the hell just said that? The one and only me, that's who? Was this a limiting belief I had that I was not aware of, or worse, was holding me back? Well, well! Nice job, unconscious mind. My point being when you allow yourself the permission to flow with your thoughts with freedom and no judgment, you might be just as surprised with what comes up.

I encourage you to explore this concept. There is no right or wrong way to do this. I want you to first find time to do it. Then feel into it and what feels right to you, your body, and mind. Again, no right or wrong answer here. Center your being and then trust what will come. Process what comes up and adjust from there. This is how I found my certainty. I hope you find yours soon if you haven't already.

Profound gratitude to my new-found soul tribe/family. Find your center, unleash those dreams, and find a tribe that unapologetically and fiercely supports you. It was the only way to my certainty. Why not try it for yourself. What do you have to lose? I kindly remind you, if your dreams don't scare you, they aren't big enough. I guarantee you will find a part of yourself you never appreciated or knew. Better yet, the best version of yourself and loving every delicious part of you relentlessly.

About the Author

Guinevere, also known as Jennfer Smith, was born and raised in Buffalo, New York. She resides in the Charleston area of South Carolina. She has overcome many mental obstacles as well as abuse, emotionally eating, autoimmunity, and self-sabotage. While using the same techniques to pull herself into the light and live the best life she can create, she helps others do the same. Jennifer enjoys working with clients who have experienced domestic violence or autoimmunity health issues to help heal them from this trauma. She has been able to eliminate her limiting beliefs and self-sabotage to go on to become a mindset coach, motivational speaker, and author. She has created a 1:1 program that concentrates on self-love and self-care called Unstoppable Love. She is currently working on her first solo book also called Unstoppable Love as well as a podcast by the same name.

Email: guineveresmith11@gmail.com
Website: www.guineveresmith.com
Facebook @Jennifer Stellrecht Smith
IG @ guineveresmith1
Tiktok @ guinevere.smith
Pinterest @ guineveresmith

Cally Tran

CHAPTER TEN

A LITTLE GIRL IN THE BIG WORLD

I remember when I was six. I loved to climb and be a bossy leader to my four-year brother, Jeelen. We would often play outside with the neighbors' kids and come up with all sorts of different games, from hide and seek to role-playing as mum and dad. Life was so much fun, playful, and carefree at that time. Mum was always busy, so Patrick and I would be best friends and create games to keep us entertained.

This little girl, on the surface, looked like she had a carefree, fun, and happy home. However, there was something more happening at home for this little girl, and it wasn't always fun and games.

Mum was always sewing. She would be awake at 4 am sewing until midday, and then she would be sewing again. All I saw her do was sit in her sewing nook with her back towards me and every so often dash away to cook and back again; she was with her back towards me again. She seemed never available as a mother because she tried to make money to support the family's living. It felt like it was always a hard push for money, and it never seemed like we had enough.

During those times, I would be playing and drawing with my brother. Every time I tried to show her how creative I could be, it didn't seem like she cared, and she wouldn't even turn around to see what I made. She would just nod and tell me to quiet down.

I was very talented in sports and athletics. However, I wasn't the brightest kid in school for reading and writing. She would always get frustrated at me for not knowing how to spell or write, scolded me, and hit me on the hands and legs with the feather duster because she thought I was naughty. I thought I was dumb because of that. My hands and legs would always get bruises from the hitting, and the fear and pain of the hitting stayed imprinted in me for a long time.

Dad was always only home after work, and we spent little time playing together. He would be resting after work and reading the paper while my mum did all the other work at home.

My only best friend was my younger brother, Jeelen. No matter what happened, I knew he would always be by my side. He was the only person spending time with me, and I knew he had my back.

Then someone moved into the house and stayed in the other room. At first, everything was ok, then arguments in the house started breaking out between mum and him (Simon). He would blame mum for doing things that she didn't do, and it would always break out into a screaming argument.

I remember Simon scolding and blaming my brother and I for doing something we didn't do. He blamed us for ripping his shirt on the clothesline. He was screaming and poking us in the head, and we both burst into tears as we knew we both didn't do it.

Dad wasn't home. My mum tried to protect us and wanted to stop him from screaming at us. Instead, he grabbed one of our kid's bicycles and threw it at her and she fell on the ground and stood back up again to defend herself and us.

There were constantly these outbreaks and arguments happening between my mum and Simon. He made threats to my mum, and this home became a very unhappy and unsafe home very quickly.

As a six-year-old, I didn't know what love was. My mum rarely took my brother and I to the park because she was always so busy. Simon would agree to take us to the park if I promise to do something with him. I would quickly say yes and get excited that we were going to the park soon.

He would take my brother and me upstairs, let my brother play in the room, cover me up from seeing what was happening, and take all my clothes off. He would ask me to do few things with him and then redress me soon after. As a six-year-old, I didn't know what that was. I thought it was ok to do that, and part of me thought, that must be love because he was spending time with me and my parents hardly did.

This happened on multiple occasions. Whenever we wanted to go to the park, he would get me to do those things with him first, and then we got to go to the park after.

Then one day, I saw something on TV that changed the whole course of what was happening. I saw a lady kicking a man, and she was screaming for help in the movie. I was thinking, why was she doing that? Are men not allowed to touch females like that?

So when I saw Simon again, and he tried to grab me to assault me again, I kicked and screamed like the lady I saw on TV. I screamed for mum to help me because she was just downstairs and he stopped when he knew she was coming up. From then onwards, the sexual abuse stopped. What happened stayed a secret, and no one knew about what had happened except for my brother, not even my mother knew.

School life was a mess. I wanted people to be scared of me so that no one could hurt me. I became this bully and rebelled throughout my school years. I started smoking, skipping school, and doing drugs. I got involved with toxic groups of people. I felt like I fitted in with these groups of people because I felt like they were similar to me. For them, I know it was also an escape from reality from their real family, their past, and an avenue of escape from their current life. When we hung out, it was like we got each other, and everything was ok. I remember sitting in a circle with these groups of friends and watching people shoot up heroin. There was a girl there shooting up too. However, she was heavily pregnant. I asked her why she was doing it.

She said she couldn't stop. She tried, and it failed. There was minimal family support for her. So she kept doing it even though she knew she should've stopped. Even though I never shot up. I was around a group of people who were lost in their own life too. It was like I didn't know who I was. I was lost in trying to find my own identity and lost in finding ways to protect myself. I felt like I wasn't saveable.

Of course, at the end of high school, I didn't do well at all. I failed high school with no UAI score. People saw me as a troubled kid and didn't know what to do about me.

Eventually, as I got to my late teens, I wanted to go back to school. I wanted something different for myself. Some toxic people are always in and out of rehab, getting caught in fights, stealing, and every day, they are trying to score for the next session. I can't live that life anymore. I saw where it was leading, and I didn't want to be there anymore. I want something different for myself. I stopped the drugs and eventually stopped smoking altogether. I left my old life behind.

I decided to start fresh and decided to go back to school again.

I started off going to do a nursing course and then eventually completed a degree in nursing and then a post-graduate in perioperative nursing.

Nursing life was quite good. The money was good, and I enjoyed the job.

However, my relationships were poor. I was in and out of relationships. I couldn't find deep connections with anyone. I had a few long-term relationships that ended sourly. I didn't understand why love was so hard and complicated.

At the age of 27, my monthly periods became irregular

and then stopped, which was really strange. I went to see a specialist doctor and got some tests done. I was diagnosed with Premature Ovarian Failure, meaning I was menopausal at the age of 27. I was told it would be hard for me to have kids. I was devastated. I remember crying to my mum and thought my dreams of having children are over. My heart sunk as I really wanted children of my own. My dreams are now destroyed, and I am left childless for the rest of my life. At this time in life, I didn't know what to do. I was in a new relationship and didn't know if IVF would even work for me.

My boyfriend and I had a chat about this issue and discussed if he would still like to stay with me and do the IVF process. He decided to stay, and we both agreed to start the IVF treatment and commit to everything that is to come.

The IVF process was such a roller coaster ride... so much pain and yet so much joy.

For many years of trying, we couldn't get past the ultrasound scan. The scan was there to check if any follicles were growing after hormone injections. I cried every time because it didn't work no matter what high drug dose we used. We tried herbs, we tried acupressure, acupuncture, yoga, and nothing seemed to bring this dream of having babies any closer.

When all of the IVF issues were happening, I was introduced to a mindset coach. I have never done anything like this before or even heard what this was all about. I was told she worked with the unconscious mind and did amazing work with guiding you through your healing. She worked with the unconscious mind to clear past issues stopping you from living a fulfilled and happy life.

So I gave it a go and went all in.

I didn't know how it would go; however, the first session we had was a major release for me. She worked on the deepest pain in my life, which was the sexual abuse when I was six. I always had so much fear when facing this part of my life. I kept it a secret and didn't talk about it to anyone, to the point that I hid everything within me so that even I forgot that it even happened to me at times.

I thought if I didn't remember it or think of it, then everything is ok and well. However, that wasn't the case. My coach told me that whatever has happened in your life all becomes a memory, and it's stored in your mind and body somewhere. It's just that you use your own mind power to lock it away and not think about it. She said it takes a lot of energy to do that.

After further coaching, I found out that when I've locked my past sexual abuse away. As a six-year-old, it created a belief system that created my reality today. The way I thought about relationships, the way I thought about how love should work, the way I communicate with people, and everything!

As a six-year-old, I unconsciously created a thought process that stopped more pain and suffering from coming in and hurting me. The unconscious thought process of this little girl was, "Why would I bring a child into this world if this is what happens to a child?"

My amazing coach traced this pain back to where I decided to store all the heavy energy. Then I discovered that all that pain from that sexual abuse was stored in my ovaries. And after many years of holding that heavy energy there, I had minimal to no eggs and follicles left in both my ovaries.

That is why I had a premature ovarian failure (menopausal) at the age of 27, even when I have no generational family history of this condition whatsoever.

After a few sessions with my coach, I felt so much lighter and free. I felt this heavy weight off my shoulder. After the session, I remember walking to work and looking around at the trees, feeling the breeze on my skin, and feeling the warmth of the sun on my face. It felt so light and free. I knew that something had changed, however, I couldn't pinpoint what it was. The only thing I knew was that it felt really good, and I finally felt peace and serene.

As more sessions went on, I wasn't getting triggered so easily anymore. My emotions were more peaceful and happy, and I started to feel the real me coming back. The me that was caring, the me that was funny and happy, the me that was more understanding, and the me that was friendly. I started feeling lighter and freer each time I had a session.

After training with my coach, I started learning how to coach myself when I found myself getting triggered. I started attending personal development and spiritual events to heal every area of my life. I started a deep spiritual awakening, understanding why the sexual abuse happened to me and why no one was there to protect and love me during those challenging times. I got rid of all the anger, fear, sadness, flashback, blame, shame, and guilt that held me down from being anything more than what I was.

I started understanding the true meaning of love and stopped blaming others for what has happened to me. I started allowing more money and wealth into my life. I learned how to love myself more even when I felt I wasn't worthy or deserving. From then onwards, I saw the world very differently. I became a renewed version of myself. This new version of me happened over a few years, and every little bit of change helped me evolve as a person. I am now the stronger version of me, with my past experiences standing alongside me with great strength and support. I was no longer scared or trying to run or hide from anything.

I even had the strength to finally sit my mum down with my brother's support and told her what had happened to me. She was able to confront the perpetrator and helped me reclaim my innocence. We both received a sincere apology, and I chose to forgive and let go of all that has happened. I hugged the perpetrator before I left as I decided to choose love over hatred. After that day, it closed a massive chapter in my life. In my mind, it was like the last page of the story has been completed and now closed and ready for filing.

I placed this book on one of my memory shelves in my mind, and it's a new belief system I've created for myself that I can overcome anything. It is also a reminder that this little girl made it out with great strength and courage, and she can do anything she wishes to achieve.

After everything that has happened, I became an Inner Work Coach to help others through their sexual abuse traumas. I help people release all their pain and suffering, blame and shame, flashbacks, and memories so that they can be their true selves once again. Because when you still live with that traumatic past within you and not let it see the light, it gets trapped within you and creates an augmented reality. So instead of the real you responding to what's happening, your insecurities, mistrust, your wild emotions come out to play instead. That itself destroys relationships, connections, intimacy, friendship, career, and other areas of your life.

You can choose to be free too. Say, "Yes" to yourself and free yourself from the traumatic past. If you or a friend has experienced sexual abuse and ready to say "yes" to yourself, I can guide you through your transformation journey. It doesn't have to be hard, you just need to know how to do it, and I can show you how. Links to connect with me are in my Bio.

I am now married to the boyfriend that went through IVF with me. He eventually had coaching done too and his life has transformed in many ways as well. We both evolved as individuals and became a complete transformed couple. We can communicate well with each other, work on issues, spend time together, still hold hands and hug a lot, still explore new restaurants, try new foods together, and still love and go strong.

After 4 ½ years of trying for a baby, 8th of October 2017, our daughter, Akira, was born. She was the perfect healthy baby that was sent to us divinely at the right time.

This little girl has taught us so much, and I know now that I learned how to be a present mum and found more ways to protect her from harm.

Then on the 3rd of April 2020, another amazing gift from the universe was given to us. Our beautiful son Ren came into our world. Ren has taught me to be even more patient and never to give up on hope, and that there is always a way.

Our family lives in Sydney, Australia, close to beautiful beaches and amazing Australian nature.

And I am so glad I made that big leap even when I didn't know what it was all about. If it wasn't for that, I would still be living that old me. The me that was carrying all that emotional and painful baggage and hoping for a good life. Because you don't know what you don't know, until you know.

Take that heartfelt leap wherever you are!

About the Author

Cally Tran is an Inner Work Coach, Sexual Abuse, & Trauma Coach and it took her 25 years to realize that anything is possible in life, to know that change is possible no matter what circumstances we come from. It took her this long to come to terms with the lions in her life and to feel strong enough to face them and make changes, and she did not do it alone.

Throughout her journey, she has dealt with absent parent and neglect, physical/sexual abuse, self-doubt, deception, drugs, alcohol, and premature ovarian failure, and these are just a few things she had to overcome. Yet all of these have been part of her journey and her path to finding and loving herself.

Her life turned around when she decided to stop running form herself and face all her challenges. She met a woman by the name of Melissa who help her learn and, on her way, back to herself. By facing her lions in her life had led her to the person she is today. She is now an author, mother to a beautiful girl, married to her soul mate, and is now sharing what she has learned by helping other overcome hardships like hers.

Her days are filled with a practice of treating herself with unconditional love and respect, loving every part of her mind, body, and soul and helping others to do the same.

Cally Tran helps you resolve the root cause of the issue from the unconscious mind helping you evolve from being a Trauma Survivor to Living Love and Freedom
Website: https://www.themindatone.com
Facebook: https://www.facebook.com/TheMindAtOne
Schedule a Meeting:
https://go.oncehub.com/60minuteClarityCall

Maggie Olson

CHAPTER ELEVEN

MOMENTS WITH MANGO

Hi there, welcome to my chapter. I'm glad you're here!

My journey started on November 2, 1997. Growing up, I was always close with my parents, especially my mom. I enjoyed their company and told them more than the average kid did. I always said, "I want to have a good relationship with them when I'm older." This is a true fact to this day! Growing up, I was always a homebody; I found comfort and safety at home.

As I progressed in school, I seemed to struggle with finding and making friends that I really connected with. I had absolutely no desire to be a part of the “popular” crowd in middle school. I knew that they just weren't my kind of people, and that was fine with me.

It wasn't until high school that things took a turn. I believe I have always had anxiety, and in high school, it manifested at an extremely rapid rate. High school is a time that is a blur for me and a time of loneliness, experimentation, moments of happiness and love, extreme pain, and hard-core anxiety.

You know, the usual feelings every high school teenager experiences, right?

Along with always believing I was an anxious person and having hindsight now, I believe that it was only a matter of time before I found drugs.

The first drug I ever did was over-the-counter sleeping pills, and I was either 15 or 16 years old.

Weird choice, you might think.

I agree.

I also believed that I wasn't a very smart drug user. I wasn't savvy with drugs. I always felt like the loser, even when I was among the ‘druggies’.

So back to when I took sleeping pills the first time. If any other alcoholic or addict is reading this, you will understand the next couple of lines.

"I was sitting in McDonald's with two friends, and when one friend told me he started using sleeping pills, I had the thought, I am going to do that.

And there was never a second thought.

No "hey, maybe this is a dumb idea" or "maybe, let's dig deeper into why you want to do this." I was powerless against the first drug.

From that point on, it just progressed. The first six months of using the drug, it was alone and in secret.

Nobody knew what I was doing. I mean, why should they know? I'm totally fine.

Finally, the first incident happened and my parents caught me. I mean, it was bound to happen when my dad caught me talking to furniture because I was trippin' balls that bad!

People thought I was trying to kill myself, which was a lie. I have never been suicidal in my life, and it was a slap in the face to hear that.

People were worried about me, and instead of taking in their considerations, I was pissed. Their concerns and worries were getting in my way of doing drugs. How dare they!

Eventually, sleeping pills progressed to Marijuana, then MDMA, and then Meth.

Once I found MDMA, I thought, this is exactly what I'm going to do for the rest of my life. I felt I had arrived.

MDMA gave me the confidence and happiness I was always seeking.

It allowed me to talk to people I couldn't normally talk to.

It made me feel pretty.

It allowed me to have 'deep and meaningful' conversations, which I so desperately wanted.

It just allowed me to step out of the reality I was living in. A reality which I felt was hell.

My end goal was to graduate high school, and I just barely skid by. I felt like this was a huge accomplishment on my end! A Lot of my peers had applied to university while still in high school, and I knew early on that I wasn't going to university, not right away at least. I was not interested in wasting my time, money, or the university's time.

Once I graduated high school, that is when things really went down the toilet. I was using a lot more during the summer after graduation. My parents were gone camping, and I had the house to myself and found a guy who coincidentally was a drug dealer (weird how things line up, hey?) At one point, I left my parents' house to live with this guy.

That's right, I packed a whole garbage bag full of random shit and said, "Yeah, F this place. I need more freedom, and I'm just not getting that here. Peace out."

My alcoholism was in full force here. I was so sad, miserable, and confused. Like, how am I, Maggie, doing this when I have loving parents at home and had a good upbringing? Why am I like this right now? Who am I?

Finally, after maybe two weeks, I came home, and the three of us found a treatment center called Alberta Adolescent Recovery Center (AARC). It is an inpatient, intensive, long treatment program based on the 12 steps of Alcoholics Anonymous (A.A.). I went into treatment in October 2015 when I was 17 years old and finally graduated in July 2016 (I'm a slow learner, what can I say!) During my treatment, I had a few hiccups.

One of them was signing out for two weeks on my 18th birthday to go back to my drug dealer and then finally realizing that I was ready for this level of help. Those two weeks back out solidified that the drug lifestyle was not the one for me. The second hiccup was running from treatment. This was a very embarrassing moment for me, yet I believe it was the last piece I needed to completely reak the addiction cycle. After those two hiccups, I was fully in. I was ready. No more fooling around!

Treatment was excruciating at some points. I had to get up in front of everyone and talk about my feelings. YIKES! This sent me into a few panic attacks! Treatment taught me that even though I have these fears relating to my anxiety, it doesn't mean that it will kill me and that I deserve special treatment. Without treatment, I would be writing a much different story right now, or maybe I wouldn't be writing at all.

During the treatment process, I was finally put on anxiety medication which was truly a lifesaver. Today, medication for my anxiety is not the solution but a tool to use in my everyday life.

Treatment gave me the introduction I needed to A.A. and gave me a basis for how I should structure my life.

Once I graduated, I was an entirely different person.

I was principled, kind, easy-going, sober, not crazy, and overall just a better human to be around.

Once I graduated from treatment, I felt that life had begun.

I was excited for my new life and excited to see where it would take me!

I worked two jobs, attending meetings, hanging out with friends, and having a good time with my new life.

Shortly after treatment, I got pregnant and had my son in August of 2017.

Having my son is the greatest gift of all time. Without him, I would not be where I am today. All the opportunities I have today would not be present if I didn't have him.

I am an ever-evolving spiritual person. I believe in God, but not in the traditional sense.

I believe in a loving entity, one that is bigger than all of us and loves me in all my totality. I call my God a 'He.' I cannot describe a picture of what he looks like, but I can give you plenty of examples of when he has shown up for me. God has given me my flaws and mistakes so that I can be the person I was meant to become and learn the necessary lessons in this lifetime. He has given me my flaws so that I always turn back to him. God and I have an on-and-off relationship sometimes. This type of relationship occurs not because God doesn't care about me but because I do not put in the necessary work. His plan is always more elegant in comparison to my plan.

God gave me my son so that I could get to where I was meant to be today and to show me unconditional love in human form.

While pregnant with my son, I was doing lots of upgrading of high school courses. I thought for the longest time, I wanted to be a guidance counselor and was going to go into education at university.

That plan shifted. I decided I wanted to take a Fetal Alcohol Spectrum Disorder (FASD) certificate and then later on an addictions certificate. The FASD certificate was all online, which was perfect as I had a newborn at home! I had my son on August 24, 2017 and classes started on August 30, 2017.

It was a challenge for sure having a newborn at home with minimal sleep, yet the classes gave me mental stimulation.

The year after I started the FASD Certificate, I started an addictions studies certificate but never finished either. I knew going into them that they were not my destined career paths, and so I dropped out of college in May 2019. The next phase of my journey is conjoined, and events overlap, so stay with me!

I was looking into surrogacy a year before dropping out. I was intrigued by the idea of helping someone build a family. I thought “I have the ability to create families, so why not give someone the ultimate gift of life; a child!” I met the criteria to be a surrogate and also had the thought, "If this turns out to be a super shitty experience, then I never have to do it again."

Side note: as I write this, I'm sitting outside enjoying the sunshine five weeks pregnant with surrogate baby #2!

I matched with my Intended Parents (IPs) in January of 2019. It took us six months from meeting, doing all the necessary screening (both psychological and physical), and signing contracts until we transferred the embryo in July 2019. During this pregnancy, I was in a relationship. He was a great guy, and he treated my son and I so wonderfully. However, we did disagree on surrogacy, so he was not entirely on board and now looking back, I definitely understand why a partner needs to be on board 100%. I wasn't as excited for this experience as I know I could have been due to him not being on board. Looking back, it is a bit of an odd situation. We started dating in November 2018, and then a couple of months in, I told him that I want to carry another man's baby.

How many people can say they have been in that situation?

Probably not a lot!

Here’s where things overlap! Between the time I dropped out of college and the time I got pregnant with surrogate baby #1, I noticed my passion for birth and babies was rising. I wasn't sure where this was taking me, but I just went with the feelings. I looked into midwifery school and was appalled at the time and energy it would take to complete it. Then, one day on the train home from college, magically, I stumbled across doula work. I believe God was working his magic here as I had no idea what a doula was or that this was even a possibility!

Ecstatic was not enough to describe what I felt when I found doula work! I had never felt this passion and purpose towards a career before, and I was so excited to learn and explore this topic!

In April of 2019, I signed up for an online postpartum doula course! I knew birth had my heart, but I chose postpartum just because my son was so little, and birth was unpredictable.

I have noticed that sometimes I tend to do things that don't fully align with what my heart wants. I end up paying for things that don't fuel my soul and end up in debt or out of that money. I also end up wasting time that could have been spent on other things. Yet, in saying all that, I again believe that I would not be on the same path I am today without those pit stops. Sometimes, to find out what we want, we have to look at what we don't want first and go from there.

It only took me two years to finish my postpartum doula training, but I did it! While I have no interest in that field anymore, I am glad I finished it! As for my birth doula training, I finally took the plunge and signed up for the training in Jan 2020! Joy, excitement, and happiness took over.

I love birth. I am a huge birth nerd! If there is a birthing video, I am there for it. I want to see it all! Birth to me is beautiful, magical, and transformational. Being able to join in on a family's birth experience is one of honor and a very sacred time. It does not matter if it is a natural home birth, a C-section birth, or anything in between. Birth is birth, and I am over the moon to be able to support and hold space for their experience.

I discovered, trained, and attempted to build my doula business during my surrogacy pregnancy. While I wish I would have worked more on my doula business while pregnant, I had to honor my body and accept that it needed rest. The surrogacy pregnancy was hard on me physically and mentally, and because of that, I had to be gentle with myself.

My surrogate baby made her debut on March 30, 2020, at the start of a global pandemic! The birth was hard, but I'm so eternally grateful for the entire experience. I witnessed her dad's step into the parent roles, which completely made my heart melt. I knew this baby would be loved from day one and seeing them see their baby just reaffirmed that love. One perk out of many about surrogacy is that I get to sleep after the baby is born. I'm the cool aunt, so when the baby starts crying, I just hand them back to their parents!

After the birth, I took some time to rest and just enjoy not being pregnant.

Shortly after I had the baby, I found a business coach! I felt weird having a business coach so young. People tell me I am mature for my age, and I agree with that, yet I always felt out of place if I ever tried anything that "looked too mature" for my age.

I did it anyway despite my feelings of weirdness, and I am so grateful I did. Again, it was a building block to where I am today. My business coach was amazing. Absolutely incredible! She taught me how to use Instagram, gave me the confidence to reach out to others and slowly start putting myself out there. We all have to start somewhere, and I'm so happy I started my coaching ventures with her. She gave me the bare bones on how to start doing business on Instagram, how to create content for my page, what to say when reaching out to people, how to nurture leads, and so much more!

Once that program ended, I waited a bit until I got another coach. God definitely had a huge part in this next part. I was actively seeking out another coach, one for personal development this time. Thanks to Instagram, I found a lady in my country who had offerings I was interested in, yet the payment was not going through. No matter what I did or how I went about trying to pay her, it would not let me. Almost in the blink of an eye, I found my current coach. She commented on a post I made in a very well-known Facebook group saying she had a free workshop. I attended her free workshop, which also seemed quite odd to me. Normally I would not think much about attending a free workshop nor make much of an effort to go, but I remember I made a gentle, yet firm commitment to myself that I would attend. After I attended, I resonated so much with the content that I signed up immediately for one of her programs. When I signed up, payment went through easily and without effort. It was slick. God had a plan and was damn adamant that I stay on track.

I share that tiny piece of information with you because small moments like that confirmed that I am on the right path. If I somehow managed to wiggle past God's plan, maybe I wouldn't have gotten the necessary healing I've gotten with this coach. I'm not God, though, so I don't need to know the plan. Knowing that plan is above my pay grade. I'm grateful God has given me the ability to recognize his little "God shots" and I can gently be steered in the right direction.

Currently, I am building a coaching business. My clientele is energy workers and spiritual coaches. I support them in overcoming their own mental blocks such as fear, self-sabotage, and past traumas so that they can have a thriving business and life! While I am so early on in my entrepreneurial journey, I still feel extremely shaky and unsteady, yet I also feel this passion and excitement burning inside me. There are many feelings tied to this new venture I'm on, and I am so ready to take it all in.

Whether I think this is my final career path or not, I am 100% certain that God will show me the way. One step at a time, one moment at a time. I will always be guided along the right path.

About the Author

Maggie Olson resides in Calgary, AB, Canada with her almost four-year-old son and three kitties!

She has a passion for personal development and loves to facilitate people's transformations on their healing journey. She has training in Neuro-Linguistic-Programming (NLP) as well as she is quiet familiar with other spiritual tools that support her clients through their healing journeys. Her objective when working with clients is to help them overcome self-sabotage and fear so that they can live a more fulfilling and beautiful life as possible!

To learn more about Maggie Olson, followed her on Instagram.
www.Instagram.com/yourcoachmango

Susy E. Ramirez

CHAPTER TWELVE

ENJOY YOUR LIFE EVERY STEP OF THE WAY

It is with great pleasure that I write my history to empower women and men to follow their dreams as I am a great believer that the sky is the limit.

I came to the United States of America, specifically to Los Angeles, California, at 15 on March 20th, 1982. Originally, I'm from El Salvador, the smallest country in Central America. My immediate family consisted of my father, a bank executive back home, my mom, a devoted mother and housewife, my older sister, then it was me, my only brother, and my youngest sister.

The family on my father's side had immigrated to the USA back in the late 1940s; therefore, most of his nieces and nephews had been born in the USA. My mother's side of the family had stayed put in El Salvador, though soon after we left, most of them decided to immigrate to Australia, where they have lived since mid-1980s, and one of my aunts married a resident of Louisiana and lived there.

My father was a great provider and a professional in the banking industry in El Salvador. His family would always encourage him to come to the USA, but he felt that he, his wife, and four kids were doing well and such move would not be necessary.

We were so blessed to have had such a working father and a mother that devoted all her time to him and us. We all had a beautiful upbringing. We attended private Catholic schools, had a nice home, had a beautiful beach ranch named "Aurora Del Mar" after my mother's middle name Aurora.

I vividly remember the great times we had as a family. My father had many cousins, nephews, and nieces, and my mother had her parents, siblings, nephews, nieces, cousins still living in El Salvador, that every weekend was a trip to our ranch and theirs because they were all neighboring ranches.

We would spend every weekend, every holiday, and every vacation at our dearest Aurora Del Mar. Our lives pretty much consisted of home, school, ranch, and Sunday Mass at "Iglesia Don Rua."

Right around the year 1976, a year after I made my First Communion, which is a Catholic ritual, I became closer to God and the Virgin Mary to the point that lunches and breaks at school you would find me at the chapel located inside the premises. I would be talking to the Priest and

Nuns and wanting to learn more about my religion and God. One night, I dreamed that I was one of the girls leading a procession and carrying the Virgin Mary's statue, and she told me that I was ready to pursue my life as a Nun and serve the Lord. I woke up so happy and ready to tell my parents. I told them, and they met with the Head Nun or "Madre Directorate" of my school. They were as excited as I was, but unfortunately, I was too young then to join, but they became my guardians and mentors for years to come until I was at the right age and time to join the convent.

Fast forward to 1978, the revolution and internal political issues and criminality hit worse than ever in our beautiful country El Salvador. I remember hearing gunshots, police and ambulance sirens every day. Many times we were locked down at school. We were so afraid not to be able to see our father come home from work. My mother would protect us and keep us calm, but we often had to drop to the floor as shots were being fired too close for comfort.

My father used to drive a Ford Mustang with double bazookas that can be heard from a few miles away, so it was such a relief when we heard him come. I also remember one morning my father was driving us all to different schools, and he shouted to us, "Close your eyes and don't try to look anywhere." Well, when you are told that, the first thing we did was to look, and we saw a poor man lying dead right on the street due to multiple shots. We all cried, and that was the turning point in our lives. My father said no more, and in conjunction with my mother, decided to speak to his mother and sisters, who had been asking them to join the rest of the family in the great United States of America.

My father and mother agreed that we would not come to the USA illegally or undocumented. It took a few years for the process to be completed. Thanks to my grandmother and six aunts on my father's side of the family. On a beautiful day in December 1981, we were at the US Embassy in San Salvador, El Salvador and were approved as US residents. It was a day full of mixed emotions, especially for my parents. It was decided to sell or gift everything we owned, and we did. Now, retaking the beginning of my story, we were fortunate to reunite and meet new family members on March 20, 1982. About 25 family members were waiting for us at Los Angeles International Airport "LAX," and there must have been ten cars to drive us all to one of my grandmas' and aunt's house in LA. I remember looking out the window and thinking, "wow, we are really here." Obviously, our lives took a turn for the best, but it was a bittersweet moment for so many reasons.

I have the utmost respect for my parents to have sacrificed and make the decision to leave it all behind for the sake of their children and the wellbeing of the whole family. My father, the sole provider with an excellent career and my mother leaving her whole family behind to provide us with a secure place to live. I am honored to be their daughter, and I owe my life to God and them both.

Now think about it, we spoke no English except my oldest sister, who had attended and graduated from an extensive English course, however, had never practiced it. Needless to say, my aunts were there every step of the way and were a wealth of knowledge and information to guide us through our ever-changing lives. We got vaccinated the very next day we arrived to be able to enroll in school right away. We lived at my grandmother's house for a short period as my parents wanted us to have our own apartment.

A major change came our way. It was going from a private Catholic school to a public school system where both boys and girls attended. Shocking at first, especially when you don't even know the language and you don't have to wear uniforms, socks for moccasins. We were not sure as to what to wear but quickly got adjusted. I had already finished the 9th grade back in El Salvador, but due to timing and my age, I had to be placed in 9th grade middle school, which bothered me. However, I took it to my advantage and decided to learn English through the rest of that school year from April 1982 through June 1982. I graduated from Thomas King Junior High School with honors and spoke and understood an intermediate English level. I had decided that being a nun was no longer my call; however, I continued to serve the Lord in so many other ways.

My older sister was attending college, and she was twenty years old then. My youngest sister was in elementary school, and she was only seven years old, and my brother was in middle school or junior school back then and was thirteen years old. We attended summer school every school year; even though it was not necessary, we wanted to continue to learn English and get ahead.

I started high school at John Marshall High School in August 1982, graduated with high honors, and received the United States Presidential Award from US President, Ronald Reagan. I was top ten in the graduating class of 1985. My parents were so proud, and I was happy to see them happy and to know that their sacrifice was truly paying off. However, that is not all I did throughout my high school years. I wanted to take every opportunity presented to me. During a career day at school in late 1983, I found out about the ROP "Regional Occupational Program," which consisted of a weekly Saturday class of a career of your choice, and I decided to pursue a career in banking in honor of my father. He was so very surprised and proud that he could not hide it. I did very well in the program, which lasted one school year that I was offered to join another program called "Co Op. Banking." In this program, you would meet twice per month at a designated college for banking topics and work at a bank on a part-time basis. So my senior year of high school, I had enough credits to just attend two classes and one more as a Teacher's Assistant for an ESL class (English as Second Language), and then took three buses to get to my job as a bank teller for Security Pacific National Bank (years later acquired by Bank of America). Who would have thought that the 15-year-old girl that had come to the US just a few years ago was helping other students learn English, was working at a bank, and was a straight-A student graduating top ten of her class and receiving a Presidential Award? I felt like I was on cloud nine, yet I was doing exactly what I had planned and worked so hard for. Nothing ever comes on a silver platter; you have to dream, want it, act on it, and do it all over again to keep moving forward.

After high school graduation, I decided to attend a two-year Community College in Los Angeles named LACC, and at the same time, I was promoted to a full-time Merchant/Vault teller at another Security Pacific National Bank. I was so excited and worked there for a year when I realized that I once again wanted to focus on my studies and decided to step down to a part-time teller. Since SPNB did not have an opening for me to apply to, I decided to resign and give them my two-week resignation letter. I remind you that doing it this way is the best way to do it as you want to leave on a positive note, be able to be rehired, and never want to burn your bridges.

I focused on school so much for a week that I got so ahead of my peers. Once again, I found myself bored at home and immediately decided to call banks around my city and the first call I made was to Bank of America, Sunset and Echo Park branch where I inquired about a part time teller opportunity, was transferred to the Operations Manager and was interviewed and hired during the call. I started working there on January 21, 1986.

I was and still am a quick learner, customer service oriented, easy to get along with, and a goal-getter. I quickly grew and was promoted within the bank at multiple branches throughout my 20-year career with Bank of America. I started as a part-time teller, to a full-time teller supervisor, new accounts representative, operations assistant, assistant manager AVP branch manager, and my last assignment as a vice president and community manager in the city of San Bernardino, California. I retired on my 40th birthday on September 14, 2006, when the bank offered a retirement package once you reached 60 years between your years of service and your years of age. So I can proudly say that I am a Bank of America retiree.

I am going to backtrack a little because I have only written about my career life, but along the way I had the support of my dear parents, my two sisters, my brother, my paternal grandmother, my aunts, uncles, cousins, and a handful of great friends I had while in high school and my very best friend I met during the very beginning of our banking school days and to this date she is more than a best friend to me, she is my confidant and my go to person.

I started dating my last month of high school since I was focused on my studies and my work before anything else. I had my very first serious boyfriend at the age of 19. He was ten years older than I was as I was very mature for my age. Unfortunately, it did not last for a long time. I dated and met many nice gentlemen along the way. There was a nice gentleman whom I dated on and off for about five years, but it was not until the year 1993, when I reunited with an old family friend who is eleven years older than I am, that we both knew it was time to settle down and have a family. We got married on September 3, 1994, and planned to start a family right away. I was almost 29, and he was almost 40, so there was no time to be wasted. We became pregnant soon after our marriage, but unfortunately, I had a miscarriage about five weeks into pregnancy. I was fine, and we got pregnant very fast and had our first bundle of joy on September 26, 1995, an 8-month high-risk birth, but thankfully, she was fine, just little jaundice (a yellow coloration of the skin) that soon went away. We planned our second baby to be no more than two years apart, and our second daughter came very healthy and strong on August 7, 1997, and they are 21½ months apart. We were blessed and content with our two daughters and were so blessed to have my parents, especially my mother help us with them, giving them the foundation, the love, and respect that only a grandmother can give. The one beautiful day almost five years later came our third and last daughter born on January 17, 2002. I had a very risky pregnancy. I had gestational diabetes for eight months out of my pregnancy and had to inject insulin twice a day in my stomach until the day she was born. I never complained about how stressful that was; instead, I would pray for a healthy child as I was already 35 years old, and back then, it was very risky to bear a child at that age. Luckily our baby was well, and we were a happy family of five for a long time.

We bought our first home in the City of Rialto when our second daughter was one week old. The house was located next to my older sister and her family's house. That is where we had the best time of our marriage. We both worked hard and had the support of my parents. They took good care of our then two daughters. We were financially stable, so we traveled, we had nice cars, nice jewelry, we rebuilt the house inside and out, we provided anything and everything our girls wanted, we added a pool to the home, so it became the house to go to almost every weekend. But one day in early March 2001, my mother became very ill, and it was then discovered that she has a dime size cancerous tumor next to the liver embracing the portal vein making it impossible to operate, and she was given one year to live. Only God can decide that, but on March 26, 2002, my mother reunited with our Heavenly Father, and it was then that my life totally changed.

I became very depressed and short-tempered. I tried to hide it to the best of my abilities, but down deep inside of me, I was feeling lonely, hopeless, and missed my mother so much I would go hours and hours to the cemetery without anyone knowing. I had to be put on antidepressant medication, and I decided to pursue some psychological help, and to this day, I am so grateful I did. I was able to feel like myself again, and I learned that it is not necessary to be at a cemetery to be close to the ones you love that have passed on. I dedicated my time to my children, my household, scrapbooking, and lastly, my job. I understood the importance of my family when for so many years, I felt that I was married to my job and was happy doing so, or so I thought.

After my mother's passing, many changes came our way. First of all, my father was living by himself in a lovely home where we all lived since 1988. It had become too big for him, and it also had a pool which he loved, but we were concerned for his well-being. He was so independent that he would not allow any help until one day he decided it was time for him to find another smaller place to live in. The house was quickly sold, and he bought a new home, a Ford Mustang and kept a motor home to go on trips. Once that decision was made, all of my siblings knew that we wanted to be close to him, and we all decided to sell our homes and buy new ones near him.

We had a few more years to enjoy my dearest father until the terrible day of October 5, 2007, when my father died at the hospital where he was being checked with no known causes, but he wasn't feeling good. His death certificate indicates "unknown" as the cause of death though he had high blood pressure and diabetes but well under control. I want to believe what's always said, "People died out of love" after 42 years of marriage. I know he missed my mother dearly. I was right next to both of my parents, holding their hands when they passed on. I was blessed to have been the chosen one by God to have to go through those very painful moments, but today, I feel that made me stronger and that I can overcome anything.

We moved to the beautiful city of Beaumont,

California, where I decided to continue my Real Estate career and Notary right when the market was extremely good. I worked part-time from home for about two years. When the market crashed, and all Real Estate activity slowed down and many people lost their homes. Though I could have stayed home a while longer, I decided to re-take my banking career and joined an international bank that I will omit the name.

From July 2009-December 5, 2015, I excelled at being a Vice President and Branch Retail Executive. I have worked at three different banking centers and have been recognized as a top performer for the Inland Empire District and the only Retail Branch Executive (BRE) for the District that was recognized at events for my overall sales and service contribution and management skills that I was able to travel to Las Vegas, Vancouver Canada, Oahu Hawaii and more events. My employment ended with an absurd complaint from an elderly senile lady stating I stole $10,000 from her. I was not afraid as I knew she was mentally ill and everything would be cleared up.

Corporate Security and my District Manager knew of the situation. I thought it was all being investigated when, to my surprise, the police showed up at my office, and I was handcuffed and arrested. I thought it was a protocol to follow, and though I was humiliated, I was placed in a holding cell, and no rights were read or given to me. After what seemed to be an eternity, I was removed from the holding cell, put back in handcuffs, and transported to women's jail. I was then devastated and felt so angry and didn't understand what was taking so long to clear things up by my employer. I was released on bail, and I immediately called my District Manager, and she was so evasive and told me to stay home and rest. She said that we will talk on Monday as this was a Friday. The next morning, I got a letter from the bank's Human Resource Department stating I was no longer employed with them and attached was my final paycheck. This was so surreal to me. I thought it was just a bad dream, but it wasn't. Needless to say, I knew I had to clear my name and hired a lawyer who in one day found out there was no case against me as the District Attorney did not even file it due to lack of evidence. I have no criminal records, not now, not then, and everything was off the system like it never happened. I went through the legal channels, and you guessed it right, I won a settlement, but I must say, no monetary compensation is worth the pain and suffering that awful experience caused my family and I. Right around the same time, I knew I had fallen out of love with my then-husband that I filed for divorce. I can tell you all that my ex-husband was my best friend before, during, and after our 21-year marriage.

God has a plan for us. I decided to take a year off from everything and almost from everybody. During that year, I went to Mexico three times by plane. My smallest daughter and I took a train from California to Louisiana to visit relatives. For my 50th birthday, I went to Australia, where most of my mother's family live and my dearest cousin on my father's side of the family that I truly see as my second mother. I spend three weeks with my mom's younger sister and her husband where I was able to reunite with my cousins, I had such a wonderful time knowing how alike I am with my aunt.

In 2016, I decided to pursue some of my other talents such as human resources, beauty consultant, administrative assistant, notary services, loan signing agent, wedding official, and actress.

That landed me in a Spanish Realty show in Miami, which I was coming to for two weeks. I left the show and fell in love with the city, the weather, and all that this beautiful State of Florida has to offer that I have now relocated to the city of Margate, where I now call home.

My dear readers, I want you to know that no matter the turbulences we go through, there is always tomorrow, and the best is yet to come.

About the Author

Susy Elizabeth Escobar-Ramirez AKA Susy E Ramirez has been in the financial services for 40 years. She has mentored hundreds of associates to excel and to become the best version of themselves. As a Banker, Real Estate Agent, Certified Notary Public and Loan Signing Agent, Financial Advisor and Wedding Officiant, Susy has been able to make people's dream come true. She is very passionate about all she does and puts forth her best efforts to ensure that each client she encounters is wowed with her services. Susy's clientele continues to grow all due to referrals and word of mouth from all her satisfied clients. There is never a dull moment in Susy's life. She loves to travel at least 2-3 times per year to enhance her cultural knowledge, meet people all over the world, learn from them and sometimes incorporate her new knowledge in both her personal and professional life.

To learn more about Susy E Ramirez visit
https://www.facebook.com/susyelizabeth.ramirez.1
Instagram www.instagram.com/susyelizabethramirez
Snapchat @susyeram
TikTok @susyelizabethramirez
YouTube Susy Ramirez
Email gosusygo1@gmail.com

Chris Krag

CHAPTER THIRTEEN

LEANING INTO ALIGNMENT AND HOW TO LIVE THE GOOD LIFE

To the best of my knowledge, the world just works better when a definite purpose drives our clear intention. This happens when we are walking with certainty. How do we learn to do that? First, I believe we have to notice how much control we don't have! Next, it is important to learn that we gain certainty from having a definite intention in the first place. And then, when we can become aware of what happens when we have confidently done all we can to make our intent reality, how magic often seems to happen when we let go of the outcome.

First, whoever believed we could control everything in our world? Too many things can happen, and there is so much complexity. As we look at the crash scene, we can wonder -- what if that car in front of me had not stopped at the red light? What if I was 30 seconds later? At first glance, it is easy to think: 'Any person thinking that they can control everything is deceived,' but yet, as you can see here, we do it all the time! That insidious illusion of control sneaks up on us, and before we know it, we think all the power is in our hands. This is when we should have been able to save a loved one's life... they should have loved us enough not to abandon us—somehow, we are only good enough to fail... can you relate? I notice this, especially at times when we look back and feel guilt or shame. Let me paint you a few examples.

Today, we will focus on what control we **do** have. We will go to war, gain some dating wisdom about how powerful we are when we have a definite purpose, and talk about how to build effective support networks to reach our purpose. Sound cool? Let's go on this journey together.

Have you ever seen the irreverent, real Tina Fey movie "WTF?" I love this movie sharing poignantly about the emotional side of going to war. In "Whiskey-Tango-Foxtrot," Kim is a TV journalist filling a boring, dead-end job before 9-11. Afterword, when the networks are scrapping for anyone to be a war correspondent, she bites the bullet (pun intended) and heads over to Afghanistan, covering the war. With almost no training, Kim has zero idea what she is getting into and her life is forever changed. Shortly after arriving, Kim rides on missions with some Marines and takes fire with them, sending incredible film footage to the folks back home. Later on, she later learns that one of those guys lost his legs in an IED explosion during a mission.

Without spoiling the whole movie, Kim thinks she is somehow responsible for the influence of the story upon the missions he was later assigned, and thus, his injuries. She visits him back in America, looking for his forgiveness. His answer stunned me into (what I hope) is humility (you never really know!) "Ma'am, I lost my legs because of an IED, not because of you... let's say you are right. It is still not because of you. Some 12-year-old kid planted the bomb. Bin Laden... the Russians... the British Empire... yeah, and Kim Baker... oh ###, if you got no legs, everyone takes everything so serious. There is only so much any of us have any control of, good or bad. If you did not learn that in Afghanistan, you were not paying attention. Kim, you gotta move on. You are giving yourself way too much credit. You embrace the suck and you move the F*** forward. What other F***-ing choice do we have?" Get the point?

What happens when you get home after deployment (or your life's version of 'going to war') and (eventually), your life disintegrates? It happens in so many of our lives. That's why the current divorce rate is so high, which is just one simple example of the many ways our lives can fall apart. Then, what do you do? All you want is to meet someone great to be in your life as an equal companion and not be utterly, dreadfully alone? (This is the state we can often fall into, and it can be a death spiral. However, when you learn a few key insights, everything can change.)

Guess what I found out that the answer is to finding someone great to be in your life? You get to figure out how to date again! Yay... ok, that hit like a lead balloon. Honestly, my whole dating life was changed by the audible version of 'It's just an F*** ing date'—brought to you by the people who wrote, "He's Just Not That into You." In between bursts of laughter, I learned an amazing, compassionate truth—having a definite intention matters! As ladies, we have more control than we might think. We have direct control over our time and who gets to spend it with us (including choosing who does not get to spend time with us because they mistreat us or are simply incompatible because they are going somewhere else than toward where our life's purpose is headed). So, as we increasingly value ourselves, we understand that accepting a date is actually a prized gift that we have to offer another person—it is an opportunity for them to potentially get to know us. Then, we prepare like this is the most important date of our lives, whatever that means to us at the time. We go on the date expecting to find a great person and have fun. And then, we completely let go of the outcome. Here, we have controlled what we can, we trust the process, and then we just notice the results... we are not responsible. What happens happens—how cool is that? Learning this lesson was incredibly freeing to me. And, suddenly, I had 'great luck' in dating. It was strange, but true!

BTW---guys, this funny book can help you better understand that mystery called women... just saying. :-)

These were just two examples of how to find your place in life—in war and in dating.

So, what happens when we have a definite purpose and let go of the outcome? We start to enjoy our life so much more, and we have all of our energy available to move purposely toward achieving our destiny. Doesn't that sound like more fun than worrying and struggling? The good news is that when we enjoy the journey, it is also more effective. I think part of the reason is that we are in a great place to build effective support networks.

Support networks have been an amazing force multiplier in my life (that's what we say in the military when something causes improvements and efficiencies in stronger ways than we think it would by itself). Why is this? I often hear, "How you do one thing, is how you do everything." If that is the case, wouldn't you like to spend your life with people who help you do the right things that move you together toward a great life-, the one where you help people and see your life's purpose fulfilled?

And why does it matter what people are in your life? Another bit of current common knowledge is that you become like the five people you most hang out with in your life. I believe this is true because we catch so many things from the people around us---we either love, hate or ignore them (which can consume our life). We gain or lose energy by being in their presence. We share common attitudes, perceptions, and even gestures with them. Reflecting on my life, I have often felt that joining the military broadened my world and exposed me to a different group of generally healthy people sharing a common mission than I ever would have met staying home in South Texas.

What does this mean for you? It means that the friend who drags you down every day is doing you more damage than you ever knew. And, that positive guy you see in the coffee shop every morning and the smiling lady in the next cube over could be more important influences than you thought. The first step is just noticing how the people around you affect your attitude, emotions, energy, and even your dreams and visions.

When you are clear about whether the people around you have positive or negative effects upon you, you can just make a single choice—you can start to lean in the direction of what most helps you.

Just a quick note here about who and what you notice in your life that **does not** work for you. These are the people who drain your energy, who abuse you and take from you for their own good, or who have never learned a different, more positive way. Maybe these are the people with whom you have too much history, whom you have grown accustomed to accepting less from them than you should, where you undervalue yourself. Maybe these folks deliberately suck out your life force because they always have, perhaps they have a bad situation at their own home and cling to you to stay afloat, or maybe they do not know any better. Who knows why they drain our energy and, in the end, does it matter? Please avoid the sinkholes because they can end your life and steal the impact you were placed on earth to achieve, and ultimately keep good from the people you are meant to help.

There was a moment in my life when I learned that we each have a choice about how to live our lives, even unto death. That may sound harsh, but it is reality and a hard lesson I have learned. I am the only one who can control what happens in front of me. I can't control anyone else, and they can't really control me unless I let them. A year after I moved out of an emotionally and mentally abusive marriage, I observed the effect on a good friend when her ex-husband drank himself to death. She taught me that there are situations we can never fix for other people and addiction is one of those cases where the other person has to make a personal choice to take responsibility for the outcomes of their own life. He continually made choices that closed down his options, and he stayed with people who weighed him down and joined in his addiction.

This wise lesson saved me from excruciating pain. Two years later, my own ex-husband finished his life in the very same way. As I was processing his death and handling all the messy details that he left behind with his irresponsible exit, I found an unexpected strength and a power, which was rooted in the relief of knowing that I had truly done all I could have to help him. I also knew that I had barely saved my own life before having to leave, and I have been rebuilding ever since so that I could share some of these life lessons with people just like you.

Just before writing this for you today, I was watching YouTube, and a song I love the beat to started: Evanescence's Bring Me to Life. How can you see into my eyes like open doors leading you down into my core where I have become so numb...wake me up inside. Call my name and save me from the nothing I have become... he tries to save her from jumping off the building, and at the end, she falls away from him. Sadly, I learned that it was her choice not to be saved. And I have the same choice to make every day of my life, too.

At the end of the day, if we are not willing participants in saving our own life, there is not enough strength available on this earth to save us. Many movies have played with the concept of a rescuer being able to save the victim---and in these movies, the same storyline always seems to play out in the end. If the person has intended to make a certain choice, and they have not changed their mind, then the consequences have to play out, whatever they are meant to be.

I also find myself **asking, "Is this just the way that** this 'thing' actually works? **What is the dynamic?**" See, I often see people get stuck on an idea, who keep saying that it should be this way. They keep getting tons of resistance and feedback that their approach is not working. And yet, they keep doing the same thing. I believe it was the genius of Mr. Einstein that the definition of insanity is 'doing the same thing and expecting different results." There is a time when you have to let someone else make their own mistakes and choose to survive and thrive on another day when you have more strength. Otherwise, these people can take you out. While not always the rule, very often, the caregiver dies before the chronically ill person. The only point I am making here is to encourage you to value your own life---you only get one!

Guess what? There is good news here! When I consistently choose to lean into what feels good in my life, to invest in people who truly care about me, my world starts to shift radically.

Here is what having alignment in your life feels like, drawn from my personal experience. As you lean into what works for you, you start to develop the skill of identifying what feels right in your life. You gain clarity, and you start to instantly see the red flags marking what is not right in your life, and you simply move away. You lean toward the good, loyal people around you and you notice them treating you right. You lean into what is right. You trust and you are able to exhale, relaxing to be fully present at the moment, without exerting energy and having to constantly be ready to defend yourself. You trust your gut, and your intuitive senses get honed to notice nuances in social settings that you could never before perceive. You stop reacting and you start responding, better meeting the needs around you. As you get healthier, you do all that is within your power to treat the people in your life well, too. This ends the vicious cycle and builds a virtuous cycle, where good builds upon good, getting stronger all the time.

You begin to see where you can influence people for good, and you choose to invest that extra energy into helping other people. Here, as you live out your 'right' alignment, you build more momentum that moves you toward living out your destiny fully, one day at a time. You build great habits and you enjoy the freedom of being around people you cherish. These folks also share your values, the things you truly care about. Now, when you look around your life, you see that the people in your life love you for who you are and your world starts to open up in dramatic ways. You revel that these people now want you to be the best 'you' that you know how to be. You habitually find a new level of freedom. And you like it---life is so much more fun. You encourage your new friends and they inspire you right back. Together, you start to accomplish so much more good in the world by working as a team than you ever could have accomplished alone. That is what it feels like to have alignment in your life.

Here is a side benefit of living in alignment. When I am habitually around people I trust, I know how to filter the advice I am given. In this safe space, I become stronger, and I learn to have better judgment. I can take any kind of advice or feedback from someone I trust when I understand where they are coming from, even if the advice is challenging and hard to hear. How do I integrate challenging feedback to overcome in my life? I have learned, over time, that I need to accept permission to be honest with myself and then, seek to understand my reaction to the feedback, the feelings. It took me a while to realize I even needed an open space to process my emotions. Being in the moment and for a moment, somehow is part of learning to be fully human... and only THEN, can I determine how 'right' or on track the feedback is. By the way, I have found this process of building trust is one of the most powerful ways to build incredible friendships.

Today, we focused on what control we **do** have—we went to war, gained some dating wisdom about how powerful we are when we have a definite purpose, and talked about how to build effective support networks to reach our purpose.

How does that sit with you? Does it make sense? I wonder how you filter out the sinkholes in your life. I am curious about how you identify the good and loyal people in your life, so that you can encourage them to be more present in your life as you grow stronger.

I would love to learn more about your journey, how you got away from the abuse and mistreatment. How you are rebuilding and what courage you are finding as you learn to trust the right people again?

If you have left a bad situation where your best was not honored, and you are now finding the courage to rebuild, I can help you find your own way. Together we can discover what right treatment feels like, build and maintain support networks, and learn how to set effective boundaries out of that healthy living. As we say on my podcast, until next time, never forget that you are amazing!

About the Author

Chris Krag inspires Courageous People to live their best lives. Together, we learn to overcome loneliness by stepping out on your own freedom path and learning how to live healthier, build strong support networks & honor your own voice.

The over thirty episodes of Chris' Overcomers Quest podcast all share the real stories of people overcoming significant obstacles to build lives that work for them. And we are only getting started!

Chris served in the United States Air Force, graduated from the Air Force Academy, and retired with 6 overseas deployments. During her thirteen years living overseas, she was fascinated by how different kinds of people adapt to change and thrive. She holds BA, MA & MSM degrees, a graduate Coaching certificate, and is certified as an NLP Master Practitioner and Project Management Professional (PMP).

Often as Alpha females and empathic males, often we only need to know what to do with our tremendous energy and talent. How can we lean more into what is good, right and true for us? When we are unleashed, our natural drive, deep passion, solid ethics, and authentic sense of the world lead us where we need to go. Chris painted extensively in Europe during breaks from military life, and honed her intuitive ability to help creatives learn the essentials: what being treated well feels like (helps us can filter out the opposite), how to enjoy self-care (life is so much more enjoyable when we are good at this), how to build life-giving support networks (the secret sauce), and out of all this, how to set effective boundaries (which reserves your energy for only what/who matters in your life).

If you are ready--- to know more of yourself, to love who you are, and systematically overcome challenges so you can thrive, Chris is ready to help you start your own adventure toward your destiny.

Have the courage to take one important step and begin unleashing your inner Overcomer with Chris. You have more than what it takes inside you already. You only need the right encouragement and tools. Your life on the other side is more alive and exciting than you could ever imagine—it is waiting for you!

You can reach Chris by Facebook message at Christina Krag, follow her on Facebook or Instagram at the 'OvercomersQuest', or email her at chris.theovercomersquest@gmail.com

Lisa Shawver

CHAPTER FOURTEEN

THE MUST-WIN MINDSET

Have you ever wondered what it takes to have the mindset of a champion, a Must-Win Mindset? What is a Must-Win Mindset? The Must-Win Mindset is the ability to do what you want, with whom you want, and when you want. Having a Must-Win Mindset is the breakthrough to all your fears. It's a mindset that destroys the barriers that block you from achieving your ultimate goals. Are you ready to transform your life and achieve more?

I remember when I was ten years old. I would see lots of girls playing softball at the elementary school near my home. I begged my mom to let me play. One day, my mother signed me up for the Bobby Sox softball league, and that's where my dreams began. I was that player who only got to play the token two innings per week, in right field, no less! And you know what, I loved it! I wanted more! And I knew right away I wanted to pitch because they were the center of the action and got to touch the ball all the time.

From that first moment I stepped onto the field, there was this burning desire to become better so I could play more and even become a pitcher. Because I did not have a father, I was so motivated that I begged a family friend to play catch with me. He worked with me whenever I asked. He didn't know if I would ever get it, but he continued to work with me. I was so determined to be the best that I continued to practice every chance I could get. I think after 10,000 pitches, I finally got it! One day, it just clicked! I was a pitcher! Not only was I a pitcher, but I had done the work and learned how to play every other position too! I was willing to do whatever it took, practice more grounders, take more outfield practice, and I even played catcher. As you can imagine, that soon ended as soon as I was recognized as a pitcher. It was my burning desire that ignited my motivation to become a pitcher.

What is your burning desire? What motivates you? What do you feel is your purpose on this earth? What is it that separates the winners from the losers? My question for you is, are you currently winning the game of life? If not, that is exactly why you need a Must-Win Mindset.

It is the amount of your personal motivation that determines how much you want to succeed. If you want to be the best at something, you cannot just settle for being average. You must be anti-average.

Being a champion or the best at what you do is not just luck. You make your own luck. Those victories and lasting successes are rooted in a deep and powerful motivation to be the best. An inner desire drives you to greatness and keeps you dedicated to reaching your full potential. Give it your all. You must do whatever it is you do like it's your last time. When you do this, you will awaken an inner fire, a desire. And that desire is what propels you to become the best that you can be. It motivates you, and it is the driving force that keeps you focused on your vision and actions.

Now, if taking action was as easy as it sounds, there would be no need for this section of the book. But it isn't, and we need to talk about the barriers that prevent you from following through on your goals.

So, what gets in the way of following through with your big plans?

You may have considered your mind.

We get so concerned about reaching our aspirations that we overthink situations, which can freeze any forward momentum. We also might doubt ourselves or suffer what has been termed "upper limits." Just as you can condition your mind with positive and negative thoughts, so, too, can you get so comfortable living your life a certain way or in a particular lifestyle that you can actually prevent forward movement.

Let me explain. We'll assume that the most money that's ever been in your savings account is $10,000. Now, if you want to make more money than that, but you have not done the mindset work to get comfortable with that amount, then you will find ways to spend anything over the dollar amount where you are comfortable. If you make

$20,000, you will find ways and justify reasons to spend $10,000.

Our minds, when left unattended or uncultivated, can cause us to behave very strangely.

When you get uncomfortable either because you are on the brink of a huge change in your life or because you can feel your emotions bubble up under pressure, recognize that you are 1) struggling with upper limits, and 2) that you are freaking yourself out. In these circumstances, it helps me to have a plan for how I will combat these challenges. If I struggle with upper limits and feel like running away, I know the remedy and I practice it. It's so easy, you can do it!

Do you want to know the big secret? It's to pause and reflect. Don't react to the need to tear everything apart and abandon all your hard work. This is what you wanted, after all. Instead, sit with the feeling and get used to what you have created or how far you have come. When you relax without rushing into any action, you will realize that you can handle this next level. If I am battling feelings of overwhelm and worried about performance when I am trying a new thing, for example, then I revert to that plan. I focus on the action. I get into my body and out of my head. If I am training to do something strenuous, then my laser light is trained right on the goal. It is trained on the commands I am giving my body to perform. I do everything I can to become automated, action only, and no feelings. This is not to say that I won't ever have feelings about what I am doing. Particularly, if it's a big achievement I am staring down, then I will make sure that I allow myself to feel the emotion later—when it makes more sense and won't impede my progress. When we decide to reach a goal, we might land on the first whim that enters our minds. We might set the bar too low to ensure that we can definitely hit what we want. I urge you to reconsider this approach. Don't set what's easily attainable. Conducting yourself in this way tells you nothing new about yourself and lets you get away with believing you have accomplished something great, when in fact, it wasn't a reach. The reason we set goals, to begin with, is to challenge ourselves. That's the whole point.

I subscribe to the theory that you should set lofty aims for yourself. And if what you have identified that you want to do is so far out of the realm of where you are currently, then it's helpful to make mini-goals to reach the mammoth goal. You can use the mini-goals as stepping stones that will lead you down the path to your destination. It's reasonable to have 4-5 smaller goals that you need to hit before reaching the end result. But you might have more or fewer steps than that. I wouldn't recommend having 20 steps, for example, because then you likely need to set a smaller end goal. But if you know that you can double your business in six months, for instance, then write down the 4-5 steps that will take you there. It doesn't make sense to push a goal so far out that you can't reach it either. Set your goals to challenge where you are currently so that you have to work for it and use your mind. Set your goals so that you can visualize reaching them, but within a reasonable time.

If you don't achieve what you set out to, that's okay; keep working. Keep returning to the tasks at hand that will carry you along. Setting a goal isn't about setting it and forgetting it. It's not about setting a goal that is far out of reach, and it's not about taking action once or twice, or even massively undertaking action, failing, and then ditching your goal forever.

You are learning what works and what doesn't as you progress. You are repeating the steps that you need to if something goes astray, even if that something is you.

You are going to be challenged as you work to level up. That's just a fact of life. So, don't be afraid of failure. Try again and hone the steps that are giving you traction.

Have you ever heard about the three Rs: Review, Revise, Repeat? This is obviously pretty self-explanatory. 1) Review what you have done. Review your work. You want to assess what is working and what isn't. Be honest as you complete this exercise, or you won't get very far. If you aren't honest, you won't have any idea what you need to work on. Having nothing to work on because you deem your efforts perfect is not the truth of the matter. Every single one of us has to work on improving ourselves in some area. And if you don't have anything to improve, then as the saying goes, "You waited too long." It's exciting to know that there is room for improvement in your life because that means you will get better and become even more of an expert. That means that if you have not achieved your goals yet, then you are really close.

Once you have honestly answered what needs work, then 2) revise your approach or strategy. If you are having a challenging time getting a pitch over the plate, ask yourself, what can I do differently? Do you need to consult with an expert or coach to tighten your stance? What can you change? Revising also serves as issuing a sort-of test. You are trying new things and seeing what sticks and what is improving your results.

That brings us to 3) Be an observer of these new efforts and then practice them over and over again. Fine-tune the consistency so that you can better gauge if the new strategy is working. Keep doing this for a specified period until it's time to start over with one. While you are repeating, this is not the time to change anything (the revisions) you have implemented. This can be a very challenging part of this 3-phase process, but you must let the unedited results flow into you. You want this information. And knowing what you should not do is priceless because it provides a direction for you. This is your process screaming, "Don't go this way!" When else would you ever receive such specific advice that is tailor-made just for you? Take this data and scratch that option off your list. Execute these three steps consistently in your business and when you are trying to reach your goals, you will continually improve with each cycle. After all, it's foolproof. You can see what's wrong, and so you will never do it again. You have no choice but to get better!

I applaud you for daring yourself to be better tomorrow than you are today, and I want you to have a blueprint for success that you can take with you wherever you go. Start identifying and tackling the mini-goals and major goals you hunger for, then create your plan to support yourself using what we talked about in this chapter.

You will set yourself up for success by giving yourself actions to reach your goal.

It is incredibly powerful to do this by visualizing yourself achieving what you want in life. This is why pro athletes dedicate part of their training time to training their minds.

You cannot reach your destination without having the confidence that you can see yourself doing it. Visualizing yourself winning in whatever game or aim you are participating in is easy. The hardest part is the preparation that leads you to practice this habit.

We are wired as human beings to be vigilant of risk. There are specific physiological functions that kick on in our body when we are in danger or when we are on the precipice of taking a risk. This is what you are up against. But don't worry. Everyone is up against this obstacle. And there are ways to defeat this negativity.

How do you believe in yourself when you don't feel confident?

You take it one thought at a time.

You use replacement internal responses to combat the negative conditioning you have trained your brain to use.

Here's an example:

If you start thinking about your goals and your potential to achieve them, and you come up against a thought like:

That's crazy! I know I can't do this.

I want you to substitute that response. Try this one or one like it instead.

I am so excited to accomplish this goal. I know I can do it.

The idea is when you start considering trying something new to prime your mind to respond in a way that is more beneficial and supportive, you will have far greater success.

The other action you can take is to pause your thoughts. I liken this approach to when you are searching for something to say and that's when the "ummms" pour out of our mouths. It is helpful to stop instead of trying to fill the silence—whether you are intent on speaking or replacing a derogatory thought. Just let the silence be. Hold onto it for a beat. This is you engaging in a pattern interrupt. This is you breaking the cycle of defaulting to self-deprecating thoughts.

You will not nail this on the first try, but this exercise is not about perfection. It is about giving you an activity to do that you can work on and get better and better at.

Once you are well-seasoned to intercept those game-stopping thoughts, then you can visualize. You won't feel silly. You will feel empowered, and this is exactly the mindset that we are going to leverage.

It helps when I go to a quiet place where I feel safe and secure to visualize without any worries of being interrupted. Any interruptions can take the form of people walking in or even bad memories that you want to escape. If your daughter just left for college, for example, and you struggle with being sad when you are in her room, that will not be a good place for you. Likely, your thoughts will revolve around her, what she is doing, and how much you miss her.

You want complete and total detachment from any emotions except those that empower you and welcome abundance.

Once you have found your spot, get into a comfortable position. Make sure you're not too comfortable because you don't want to fall asleep! The same rule holds true for meditating, by the way.

Now, close your eyes. Let your mind sharpen its focus on your goal. For our purposes, let's assume your goal is to close that monster deal you've been dreaming about.

It's important to get the details right in your visualization. Where are you? Who are you talking to? In what method are you communicating? Are you speaking on the phone, texting, on Facebook or email? Are you in person? What other elements of your dream need to be true? Do you need your prospect to have made up their mind? What is your feeling as you close the deal? What do you feel as you hear the words that the prospect wants to move forward? What are they saying? "Let's do this." "Sounds great! Send me the paperwork." Insert whatever phrase or quote you think will happen and that you can hear in your head.

I like to cover the five senses when I am visualizing:

1. What am I hearing?
2. What am I touching?
3. What am I smelling?
4. What am I tasting?
5. What am I seeing?

Add your emotions into the visualization as I mentioned earlier. What does it feel like when you hear the magic words, it's a done deal? Can you anticipate that the deal is going to close? How amazing does that feel? Allow yourself to sink into all the emotions and fully experience the joy of winning this particular goal.

Get excited! You have taken the steps you needed to take to help you accelerate. It's okay to feel a wave of positivity or abundance wash over you. I love that feeling. It seems like there isn't anything I can't do at that moment!

Puppy trapped under a car? I got this!

Marketing snafus? Out of my way!

And you can insert in your mind whatever you want to resolve. That's the beauty of our minds! When we unleash their true potential, we can make anything happen, and we can accomplish anything!

End your visualization session on a high note! You did it! Whatever it was! The feeling of triumph is rocking your body and lighting up your senses! After all that hard work, revel in it.

Then open your eyes, and with that vision fresh in your mind, conquer!

With these tools, you are on your way to having a Must-Win Mindset. For more strategies to become the champion of your own life, find me at www.MeetLisa360.com.

You are full of potential, and it's time to take action and be certain. It's your choice to live the life you deserve and having the right mindset will allow you to achieve whatever you desire.

About the Author

Lisa Shawver is a former Olympic and professional athlete and founder of the Champion's Mind. She is an educator, coach, author, international speaker, and DogMom to the canine internet celebrity, @OneUpMax. She is a Mindset Empowerment Strategist and helps people just like you increase confidence, drive, and empowers you to achieve your full potential through her uniquely designed system called the 5 Rings of Success.

Lisa Shawver shares strategies and her mastery of the mind and how YOU can use her techniques to create the life you deserve and get more health, more wealth, and more success!

To learn more about Lisa's upcoming events and connect with her on any of her social media, go to:
www.MeetLisa360.com.

Pamela Grant

CHAPTER FIFTEEN

WALKING WITH CERTAINTY OF CHARACTER

The courageous lion stands at the peak of the mountain top and roars as the wind brushes through his mane. Steadfast, looking out over the ravine below him. The image of confidence and unwavering strength. The Lion King is one of the ideals of strength, poise, and ability. Disney sure knows how to send the message– think of Gaston from Beauty and the Beast. Not only does he think he is great, but also the sidekick LeFou and the whole town believe his message. He is charismatic, winsome, capable, and can even decorate tastefully with antlers. The rest of Hollywood has the same message too. G.I. Jane, James Bond, and Rocky work hard, sending us the message of "believe in yourself and win!" I grew up with all these stories and always wondered how I could have a life like them.

~MOM~

Growing up, I watched my mom work several jobs to obtain her higher education degrees and to create a safe home life. She juggled work, school, and three girls who were small and challenging. When there was no one to watch my younger sister and me, my mom would take us to work with her at the shoe store in the local shopping mall. I loathed those times because I was not old enough to do anything fun or to be able to help. I just sat there on a metal stool, wishing the hours to pass quickly. It was as exciting as watching paint dry. I was shocked one day when Mom pointed out of the window and told us she also worked at the jewelry store across the way. I did not know how she could have two jobs and go to college at the same time. Now I fondly think back on this time and wonder if she realized that in her suffering, she was teaching me valuable lessons about character that would later guide me.

~DAD~

My dad was always a hardworking man. He started his professional career in the United States Navy. In his twenties, he injured his back, which would give him pain and suffering into later years of his life. In my formative years, he would travel from town to town repairing essential equipment for businesses, such as photocopiers and cash registers. Perseverance under pressure is something I always admired about my dad. He has true grit, and this taught me to endure and to never give up, no matter the situation. He also taught me to do things with honor. Dad's love was shown to me consistently through my teenage years. He never missed a band concert or school sports game. Dad was always there, even though his job entailed a lot of driving. He always made it back in time for me! I knew I could count on him.

~ME~

Growing up, I never saw a career path that I wanted to pursue. I envied my younger sister; she seemed to always be interested in different careers. I always thought she was so lucky to have ideas about what she wanted to be when she grew up. I never had these thoughts or desires. One particular written assignment in middle school seemed to confirm my fears that I would never figure out what I wanted to do in life. My teacher required her students to write reports on what universities and majors we would choose once we graduated from high school. I froze-- I had no idea what career I wanted to pursue. My mom encouraged me not to worry about it and told me that I did not need to know what I wanted to be until much later on in life. I believed my mom, but still, the assignment plagued me. I wanted to be successful at the assignment and in life. I started believing the lie that I would not be fruitful unless I knew what I wanted to be when I grew up. This was the early 1990s before the internet was used for public purposes. There was no way to learn about different careers by going online. Back then, we could only learn about other career options by knowing people who could share this information. Our teacher encouraged us to go to a college and career fair to learn about different majors offered by universities.

Hesitantly, I went by myself. As a thirteen-year-old, I was nervous and did not know how to talk about what I wanted in a future career. My nerves got the best of me, so I grabbed a couple of pamphlets and left. I wrote my assignment about being an engineer. It was torturous for me, and I agonized over writing about a career I did not quite understand. I did not want to lie, but I knew I would fail if I said I did not know what I wanted to do. Instead, I wrote what I could from the information on the pamphlet and pretended it was a make-believe assignment. This tortured feeling followed me through high school. I could not shake the feeling that something was wrong with me because I was not certain of my path forward.

~~~

Until the primary author selected the title of this book, I had never mentally or emotionally processed the uncertainty I felt about my path in life. I pursued various university majors and career paths, obtaining a few different degrees and certifications in the process. Even still, I was uncertain of my direction, had no concrete or clear path ahead of me, and no definite map to follow. I was truly interested in and liked some careers, such as massage therapy. I chose others because I needed to make a decision and found value in them, such as business administration. Somehow, all of these paths have come together to weave a set of skills and abilities that are unique to me. This writing process has elicited soul
~~~

searching for me. I wanted to write this chapter to share my faith in God with all who would come across this book. In the process, I found myself confronting of the lack of certainty in the decisions I have made in life. However, upon deeper reflection of my beliefs, I am reminded of what the Bible says in Romans 8:28 “that in all things God works for the good of those who love him”.

While writing, I found myself asking questions such as: What does it mean to walk with certainty? Does it mean I am actually certain in the decisions I make? Of what have I been certain in my life? I wrote a list of all the certain things in my life that related to making and achieving goals. I was able to think of a grand total of two items to put on my list. I froze as if I was in middle school again, facing a giant much larger than me. I did not feel courageous or stalwart like the Lion King. Avoidance kicked in, and suddenly all the other problems in my life became bigger than the need to write this chapter. Stress from the long-term COVID-19 lockdowns, an angry and threatening neighbor, and extra assignments at work all took precedence over this project. I had all the excuses as to why I could not write the chapter; I recoiled from digging deep into what the chapter surfaced about myself. I decided everything was too difficult. I needed to try to get out of the project. I tried to recruit my older sister, another contributing author in this series, to take my place. She could not participate in this version, so it forced me to do the difficult internal work of exploring these parts of my life that I had been ignoring.

Reluctantly at first, though now grateful, I started digging deeper. With the help of a couple of good friends and my husband, I realized that I felt judged by what I saw as the world’s definition of success and certainty. Deep down, I still felt like my middle school self-positive I would fail if I admitted that I was not certain about my path in life. I believed that if I did not know what I wanted, I could not be successful or seen as valuable. These were lies buried deep inside my subconscious mind. It was a several-month process to identify these as lies. Once they were exposed as such, I knew I could heal from these experiences by applying the truth of my value in Jesus Christ, as described in Ephesians 1:4 that *"God chose us before the creation of the world to be holy and blameless in His sight"*. Through this soul-searching, I realized that even though I have not been certain in my specific path, I am certain of the character that I want to maintain while on my path. The development of these character traits started when I was young while watching and learning from my parents.

Reflecting on the experiences watching Mom at work, I wondered what it was that guided her. Did she know what it was that drove her daily? She knew that higher education was important and saw it as a way to provide for her three young daughters. She worked with determination to improve her position in order to give us a good life. Still to this day, I do not understand how she had the energy or perseverance to work several jobs, go to school and raise us girls. Another memory comes to my mind of when Mom worked as a secretary at a law office. She brought my younger sister and me to the office on a Saturday. I grumbled going there because I knew it was not going to be any fun. Mom sat us at a little table in a file room that had only one small window. She tried to make it fun by bringing coloring books and other activities to keep us occupied. Ah– how times looked before technology when parents had to be more creative to keep their kids entertained!

There was a seriousness and expectation of good behavior when we went to work with Mom. Even though I knew she struggled, she did what she had to do without complaint. I remember sitting in that file room one day, and my mom said, "Pam, no matter where you work, no matter what your position is, you be nice to everyone. Those are the people who will open the doors for you." To this day, I think it was probably because someone had treated my mom poorly, starting in what some may call a position at the bottom of the ladder. I admired this about my mom. She worked hard and held her head high, no matter what position she had.

Eventually, Mom achieved her Master's in Social Work degree by taking part-time weekend classes all four years that I was in high school. She had a desire to help other people and had a small counseling practice. She also worked for Hospice until she was diagnosed with stage-4 colon cancer at the age of 46. Mom worked hard throughout her life and tried to make life better for others. She always turned her challenges into success stories. For example, she smoked for years and suddenly stopped one day in 1980 when a woman in our local shopping mall kindly asked her to quit smoking because it was bothering her. (This was the same mall where Mom later worked two jobs.) Mom immediately put out the cigarette and never picked one up again. In later years, she became a Smoke Stoppers instructor and used her experiences to help others quit smoking. In this experience, she showed me how to pass on compassion and respect to those around me.

All praises belong to the God and Father of our Lord Jesus Christ. For he is the Father of tender mercy and the God of endless comfort. He always comes alongside us to comfort us in every suffering so that we can come alongside those who are in any painful trial. We can bring them this same comfort that God has poured out upon us.
~2 Corinthians 1:3-4 TPT

Looking back on early memories with my dad, I remember a lot of joyful times and feelings of safety, as well as some difficult lessons that he taught me. Overall, he had a great balance of letting small mistakes go and being stern when it was something really important. That combination of loving correction made me listen really closely when he wanted me to change my behavior. From Dad, I learned many good character traits. Some of these are having a high regard for honesty, integrity, keeping my word, and helping anyone in need.

One of the lessons my dad taught me was perseverance in my work. I can remember my dad and me sitting on his sofa working on my math homework. Even though he had been out of school for several years, he sat there with me while I struggled to complete the problems. At times, there were problems that the teacher gave us for homework that she had not taught us. There we sat, Dad and me, side by side, as he persevered trying to instruct me. I would often get frustrated when my dad could not explain something immediately. I had an unfair expectation that he would immediately know how to solve every problem—after all, he was my dad and should know these things. I would feel my frustration grow and my dad would tell me that I needed to be calm. My dad's demeanor and perseverance with my frustration showed me love and compassion. I hold that dear to me now in adulthood.

Several years later, I had a friend who needed my help working through a math problem. I sat for over two hours trying to remember how to solve it. In the end, after much memory searching, contemplation, and calculation, I succeeded and solved it. My friend commented that I had a lot of determination; I had never thought of it like that before. The experience reminded me of the times my dad chose to sit beside me, working on similar problems. From Dad's example, I learned to push through and persevere with patience.

You need to persevere so that when you have done the will of God, you will receive what he has promised.
~Hebrews 10:36 NIV

From my parents, I started to learn about the certainty of character. I chose to ignore that for a time and rebelled because others hurt me. Now, my path as a Christian is building on the early foundation by teaching me to put character and relationships above outcomes. Some would call this process-oriented rather than goal-oriented. I still care about the end goals; I just care much more about how I get there.

There was a time in middle school that I was afraid because of repeated bullying. At some point, after the bullying stopped, I became angry and defensive. I was afraid to be bullied again, so I acted like I stopped caring about people. I did not have the words to express myself at the time—I felt confused, scared, and left out. My heart hurt. It seemed as though the more I tried to have friends, the more I got hurt, so I stopped trying. The cycle continued into high school and I missed out on the chance to make many long-standing friendships. Instead of knowing how to resolve differences and restore relationships, I made choices that ended up hurting myself and other people. This continued into my adult life; I still experience some lingering effects. Hurting other people left a pit of worry in my stomach. It seemed as though I could not go through a day without saying or doing something to upset someone. This created conflicting feelings inside because I wanted to treat people well. These feelings eventually grew into a huge lack of self-confidence, feelings of condemnation, and unforgiveness for myself and others.

As a young adult, I was so full of confusion about the wrongs I had done, that I felt I could not possibly be forgiven. The words of Romans 8:1 teaches *"there is no condemnation for those who are in Christ Jesus".* This did not make sense to me. It sounded nice, but I never felt true forgiveness for mistakes in my past.

It was not until 2011 while on an internship trip to Peru that I felt like I experienced true forgiveness for mistakes that I made. This experience opened my heart to be more forgiving of others. Since then, the most helpful reflection on forgiveness has come from Bruce Wilkinson's series: *70 X 7: Finding Peace by Forgiving Others...And Yourself.* This online course helped me see the weight on my mental, physical, emotional, and spiritual health that unforgiveness has on me. It also taught me a deeper meaning behind Jesus's approach to forgiveness.

> Then Peter came to Jesus and asked, *"Lord, how many times shall I forgive my brother or sister who sins against me? Up to seven times?"* Jesus answered, *"I tell you, not*

seven times, but seventy-seven times." Matthew 18:21-22 NIV

In the series, Bruce Wilkinson describes something called the "forgiveness verifier" to see if there is unforgiveness in a person's life. He asks, "Would you say you experience torment from time to time?" My answer was "yes" to having feelings that felt like torment. Before this course, I called it "worry", or "butterflies in my stomach", or "sleep problems". Going through the course, I started being able to release myself and others from my internal prison. My unforgiveness, mainly for myself, was keeping me from being in loving relationships with people.

It has taken me time to learn God's grace and how to forgive myself and others. However, it is still a challenge, but I evolve, learn, grow, and work to show patience. I have hope as I walk with God into the valley. I understand that God's grace covers me and I respond to that by acknowledging my sin and asking for forgiveness. Over the years of following Christ, He has changed how I see myself and He is the source of my certainty. It is not about making or achieving goals, although they are nice to have. My priority each day is to make a genuine connection with the people God has put in my life. I try to remain vigilant and open to these interactions to help and to receive help from others. I am far from perfect, and when I am in a rush or have a tight deadline, it is easy for me to slip into old habits. However, I do not feel condemned for my mistakes and I no longer need to be ashamed or defensive.

Therefore, as God's chosen people, holy and dearly loved, clothe yourselves with compassion, kindness, humility, gentleness and patience toward all. Be gentle and

humble, unoffendable in your patience with others.
~Colossians 3:12 NIV/TPT

These deep feelings of humility and compassion have been growing through my study of the Bible. I no longer ask myself if I am like the lion on the mountain top. Hollywood is no longer my ideal of how I walk with certainty. Upon closer reflection through this writing journey, I have come to a conclusion. I *do* stand with certainty. This world will pass away, but God is building something that will endure forever: my character. Whatever path He has me take in the future, I am safe in the certainty of Christ.

For we are God's masterpiece. He has created us anew in Christ Jesus, so we can do the good things he planned for us long ago.
~Ephesians 2:10 NLT

About the Author

Pamela Grant grew up in Upstate New York, USA, and currently lives in British Columbia, Canada. She was a Licensed Massage Therapist for 15 years and now works as a public health professional. Pamela has volunteered her time and completed internships in Peru, Argentina, Guatemala, and Liberia. She is fluent in Spanish and loves to meet people from different cultures. In her free time, she enjoys taking walks and going on bike rides with her husband, Mark. She also enjoys singing, playing the guitar, and sharing the love of Christ with those around her.

For more information contact: Email:
717girlproductions@gmail.com

Cesar R. Espino

CHAPTER SIXTEEN

GROW THROUGH IT

Life is full of adventures and secrets... things you do not expect, things you do not understand, and sometimes these things can take the best out of you. And it is during these times, you have to go back and look deep down and ask yourself, am I **walking with certainty**?

So, what is certainty? And why is this an important factor in your life's journey?

According to the dictionary, certainty is defined as a *firm conviction that something is the case*, or is *the quality of being reliably true,* is *a fact that is definitely true or an event that is definitely going to take place.* While all of these are true statements of *certainty,* I want to give it more weight by letting you know that walking by certainty can be seen as walking by faith or walking with purpose.

This book couldn't have come to me at a better time in my current life journey. As I was thinking of what would be the subtitle of this next volume of the book series, *You Can Overcome Anything,* I came across some challenges in my life's journey. And with some of those challenges, I was reminded of the certainty of my faith, the purpose in my path and my life's journey.

One of the few challenges I was faced with was all within my own self, challenges related to a long year of financial challenges, emotional challenges, and relationship challenges. I also learned that I am not alone as this was a part of many other people's challenges during a year that forever change the history of humankind, the era of Covid-19 or the year 2020. There was no doubt that this was a challenging time for many, and it was rewarding for others. After evaluating and thinking back on the series of events, and for that matter, any events from this point forward, the one thing I must focus my time and attention is how I react and what I do about the circumstances. As my mentor, Marshall Sylver will tell me, *"Deal with what emerges."*

Realizing that I was going through some financial challenges, emotional challenges, and relationship challenges was so important to the process of helping me get back on track. And all of this looped back to my certainty, my purpose, and my faith. See, when you have a clearly defined purpose and walk with certainty, no matter how difficult the situation might be, you will push through and continue to march forward because you are staying true to your purpose and your certainty. In addition, as I think of my financial challenges, what came to mind is that I am on this journey to make a difference. Further, I enjoy every step I take along the way, even if I do not see immediate financial results. You must understand that if you are working for profits, you are doing it wrong; you have to be working for a purpose.

"Follow and strive for your purpose, not your profits."
~ Cesar R. Espino

Here are four things that I took away from the many challenges, and they all fall under these four ideas, which can help you in your own life challenges.

1. Take responsibility – At the end of the day, it does not matter what took place or who did what, or whose fault it was, you must take full responsibility of the situation to impact its outcome. Because regardless of the situation, you are the only one that has full control of its outcome, and that is through taking full responsibility.
2. Acknowledged – As difficult or not so easy it may be, you must acknowledge and have a clear understanding of what is taking place or took place. Acknowledge to surrender, and you are not surrendering to give up, you are surrendering to understand, recognize, and be at ease and peace to create a new foundation and start building a new outcome.

3. Learn from it – At the end of anything we go through, we must learn from it. A lesson that we must extract from that challenge and situation is that recognizing that from those challenges, from that pain, there is a purpose, and we must learn from it.
4. Grow from it – Do not just go through the many challenges; you must grow from it, not just go through it. Even when we are faced with unwanted challenges or situations, our first desire is to get through them as quickly as possible to move on to the next thing. However, instead of rushing it or wishing it was over, learn from it, grow from it, and extract the lessons that will ultimately help you move to the next thing in a more focused and certainty-driven aspect.

"When you keep pushing forward and have faith, you can do more than you thought!"
~ Cesar R. Espino

Implementing these four ideas certainly help me to keep pushing forward, yet it was not easy, and there were many internal battles I had to face. As a matter of fact, many of the battles we have to face are all inside us. Many will think that the battle is with the society, your relationships, your acquaintances, or all the external things happening around our lives or the world, where in fact the battle is within.

When there is no enemy within, the enemy outside can do you no harm." ~ African Proverb

This is a difficult pill to swallow as we do not want to take that responsibility. I am guilty of it, and so are you. As one of the four ideas, it is crucial that we take full responsibility. Will Smith said, *"It's* ***not your fault if your*** *partner cheated* ***and*** *ruined* ***your*** *marriage,* ***but*** *it is for* ***damn*** *sure* ***your responsibility*** *to figure out how to take that pain* ***and*** *how to overcome that* ***and*** *build* ***a*** *happy life for yourself."* And this is not just relatable to a love partner. This is relatable and applicable to everything in your life. It may not be your fault, but it is for damn sure your responsibility to fix it and make it better for yourself.

Well, at first, this was so difficult for me to do; although, I already knew and had practiced this in the past. It did not come easy to me. 2020 was perhaps one of my most challenging years as it relates to relationships. Why was this difficult for me? I, too and up to this date, keep asking myself the same thing, as I had previous relationships where everything seemed good, and all was lost yet I was able to recover from it rather quickly. Not this time because it was different. This was the first time that I was involved in a relationship being in a different place in my life's journey. I had taken so much time to evaluate my past relationship. I had tried so much to learn how to become a better man in my new relationship. I had done so much internal work so that everything will come out perfectly. And there is where the challenge lies, I had certain expectations, and I was blindsided by what could be versus what it was.

To say I was not heavily involved emotionally in this relationship is an understatement. Unfortunately, I gave it all, and I was incredibly involved and lost in something that

I allowed to take the best of me. This is where taking responsibility and recognizing that I was in a unhealthy relationship came into play. I had chosen for this to go as long as it did; it was the first step to bringing back my sanity. While living in this relationship and hoping that everything will work out for the best, I was in reality losing myself, I was losing myself to the point where it affected my mental, emotional, and financial health, and brought doubts of defeat upon me.

"If you are going through any challenges today, right now, this moment... know that this is just a test of faith, and how you combat and go through that challenge is the difference between winning or losing... chose winning"
~ Cesar R. Espino

This relationship affected me emotionally in many ways. To really think about it, it was not so much the relationship as it was my own self allowing the series of events to occur both in the outer world and the inner world. What I mean by this is that the outer world or external world, all the things happening outside and around my life, were all a direct reflection of what I allowed, and most importantly, the inner world or what was taking place inside my head that reflected all around.

This comes to my next point where I allowed an external factor to affect my mental health and way of thinking. I temporarily lost touch and focus on what was my purpose and the certainty in my life's journey. The emotional rollercoaster was one of those where I started doubting myself. I felt lost, I felt defeated, and I felt I was not getting ahead to the point where I had so much down time due to now wanting to do anything. Because I had this constant fight within myself, I questioned every single step of my life.

I was asking myself if will ever be able to be in a loving relationship. Will I be valued? I'm I worth it? Will I be able to come out of this as a winner? Did I do wrong by leaving my well-paid job to become an entrepreneur? From this single experience, my entire life came down inside my head and had me questioning everything, not just my relationship experience, but everything in my life. The fact that we were in the middle of a pandemic and lockdown due to Covid-19 did not help the cause at all.

There were days I will come home and feel like a total failure, there were days I will go to see my dad and I was mentally drained and in tears. There were days I will go out for long hours looking and seeking an answer as to why, why me, why I was going through this and could not find the answer. And again I came to the realization that all this crap was inside my head, and I was better than that, and I had a bigger purpose. I had to go back and look deep down and find myself again and remind myself that when you walk with certainty, and you have a picture of where you want to be, there are going to be many external influences that will try to keep you off track and it's up to you whether you fall for it, or you bounce back and get back on track. It sure took me a while to get back, yet I was able to get back and was refocused again. However, this was not until after I allowed this circumstance to affect my financial life as well.

You might be asking how this affected my financial life. Well, simply put, because of the internal battles I had in my head. I've lost focus on my professional journey and created an unproductive environment which led to falling short. As dumb and simple as this might sound, I had no energy to do anything and therefore kept playing this victim card on my head and allowed that to drain me of my energy. I did not want to do anything to the point where I will sit in my office and just kill time. Some of my closest friends that have seen me grow and have seen my entrepreneurial journey said to me, "You are letting this circumstance eat you alive and are allowing it to drain your energy, and you are losing focus, you are better than this." This was an eye-opener because many people saw that I was not in a good place. Because I was not focused, I was not producing the necessary results I needed to bring in revenue and increase profits.

I was losing myself because, in my head, I was thinking, *gosh, this was a challenging year for many, including me, due to Covid-19.* I was blinded by a relationship, and the list of things kept going. Then I had to really look deep down and realized that the external factors had nothing to do with my success, my wealth, being, and my progress in life. What could make that difference was that person who I see every day (throughout the day) in the mirror; that was myself. Again, recognizing and acknowledging is one of the steps to total alignment. Another step I had to come to terms with was to take full responsibility for all the actions taking place in my life. The next part was the real shift I've needed in this journey of certainty. That shift was learning and growing from this experience.

What I did after going through all of these four stages was to use my resources. We all have resources that can help us in our journey, and it is okay to reach out to them and seek help when needed. Not doing so is foolish, and it is only hurting ourselves. We must put aside the ego and be okay to get the help that is needed. Because I have a background in NLP (Neuro Linguistic Programming) and I have worked a lot on my own personal development, I knew I could count on my own community to assist with some of my mental blocks. Again, let us face it, many of the challenges we are facing outside (the external world) are all coming from our mental blocks, and no matter how much we work on ourselves, we will always need someone to help us and guide us. Again, if you think you do not need anyone, you are hurting yourself.

"It's okay not to be okay, what is not okay is to give up during the process to greatness... you got this."
~ Cesar R. Espino

So, I did. I have reached out to my community and made some tradeoffs. I have numerous clearing around my childhood and past relationships (both loving and family relationships). For those of you who do not know I was born in Mexico City to just one parent, and I was literally broke and poor, I had gone through so many things throughout my childhood that I was not a normal kid. Meaning I started working at a young age. I had no clothes, no shoes, no house; my mom left me behind with my grandma at the age of 4 to follow her American dream. You might be asking me why this event is relevant to my recent mental blocks and my NLP clearings. Well, as a kid, our minds, specifically our unconscious minds, are more receptive to what takes place between the ages of zero and seven. If whatever took place between those first years of our lives are not taken care of or dealt with, they can follow us until our later years and as adults because they are sitting on the root of our unconscious mind and sooner or later, some of that will come out without even knowing why.

As I see things now, there are many things I did not clear or dealt with that finally caught up to me. I guess because 2020 was challenging, it all came out to light. Yup, I was poor, and I had to work very hard for my money, for crying out loud I was working as a child to have food on the table. Awe, that explains why I've lost focus and challenged my own self when looking at my financial stability. My mom and other relatives left without me understanding why. However, they left for some reasons. It was not done intentionally. They had a much bigger purpose, but to that inner child, it was difficult. As a child, I did not comprehend, yet that left a lasting impression on my unconscious mind, explaining why I had several relationships that failed. I kept staying alone, even when I do not understand completely why.

I had to come to terms with many different things to remind myself that when I want something bad enough, I must keep walking with certainty to overcome those challenges no matter the obstacles.

My message to you is that whether you are like me as an entrepreneur or working a 9-5 job, we all have challenges, and for us to keep marching forward we must know what our ultimate purpose in this life is. We must go back and look deep down, and through it all, we must walk with certainty. And in any challenging situation, we have to stop, reflect, and create a vision from that reflection, always with the understanding of what we want rather than focusing on what we do not want.

Just a few other things besides the already mentioned four things in this chapter that you can do to help you in your own journey and get you back on track with that true purpose you have.

- Focus on the power of the mind
- Be grateful each day
- Create a daily ritual or habit
- Exercise
- Always be learning, always be a student of life
- Stay true to your mission, vision, and values no matter the challenging times

And last, remember that if you are reading this book, there is a major reason why everything that takes place in your life has a purpose. You may not see it now, yet eventually, you will see how that one event in life shaped your journey. Keep in mind that if you are reading this, God, the universe, or whatever greater power you believe in, is not done with you, and there is still so much for you to accomplish in your lifetime, do not give up, do not give in; instead, give it all you have.

About the Author

Cesar R. Espino is the creator of You Can Overcome Anything! Podcast Show, You Can Overcome Anything Book Series, a real estate investor, mind coach, business consultant, and multiple #1 best international book author. His passion and highest intention are to empower, inspire, and motivate others to reach their full potential. Cesar offers a variety of tools and services to help people improve their current situation. Cesar is creating opportunities for people to have a chance at life regardless of people's background and current situation. He was recently in the international TV Show @EnamorandonosUSA by UniMas (Univision)

Pick up his latest books: At Amazon: Amazon.com: Cesar R Espino: Books, Biography, Blog, Audiobooks, Kindle
Website: www.CesarRespino.com
Podcast: https://podcasts.apple.com/us/podcast/you-can-overcome-anything-podcast-show/id1497917624?uo=4

Follow him at Cesar R. Espino | Linktree

ABOUT THE AUTHOR

Cesar R. Espino was born in Mexico City during a time where the country had one of the largest foreign debts and was going through a financial crisis. Not only was he born into a poor family, he was also born to just one parent (his Mom), and never have met his biological father. As a kid Cesar lived with his grandmother, mom, and older brother, living in a room or what he called his house that was just about 200 square feet. This place had no running water inside, no floor and lived and slept directly on top of dirt, no insulation, and was made up of sheet metal and plywood. He lived in this house holding four of them and until the age of just a few months of four years old. Around the time his mom took the leap of faith, where she decided to leave his family behind and migrated to the United States to chase the American Dream and support her family across boundaries. This became a pivotal moment in Cesar's life as this forced him to start working at an early age (at four) to just be able to survive and put some food in the table.

Throughout his life journey, he has overcome many different obstacles. Today Cesar R. Espino's passion is to empower, educate, inspire, and aspire many through his experience and life lessons. Cesar's has a Master's Degree in Business Administration, has worked for several worldwide companies, held positions in corporate America, is an Author of the Book ***You Can Overcome Anything! Even When the World Says" NO"***, is a Co-Author of the Book ***Dare to be Authentic Vol.5 Let Yourself***

Prosper, International Author of the Book ***Puedes Superar Cualquier Cosa! Incluso Cuando El Mundo Dice "NO",*** Co-Author of the Book ***How We Became Entrepreneurs, Follow Our Leads: Book*** 1, and many other books, Real Estate Investor, Real Estate Mentor, Podcast Host of the Show **You Can Overcome Anything! Podcast Show** and most importantly a son, father, and grandfather.

Cesar offers a variety of programs to help people improve their current situation, educate, and provide a way to have their own business. Cesar's is creating opportunities for people to have a chance at life regardless of people's background, and or current situation. He is able to do this through his many different programs and experiences in multiple areas.

Such areas of:

- Real Estate Investing
- Best Selling Books
- NLP (Mind and Life Coach)
- Mentoring
- Business Consulting
- Self-Development Events
- Live Public Speaking, Podcast, and News

www.facebook.com/cesar.espino.1297
www.instagram.com/cesarrespino
www.CesarRespino.com
www.linkedin.com/in/cesar-espino

Made in the USA
Middletown, DE
06 August 2021

45388907R00116